Family Num Adds Up

Lessons from the Family Numeracy Pilot Programme

nfer
National Foundation for
Educational Research

The
Basic Skills
Agency

Acknowledgements

The Basic Skills Agency would like to thank Dr Greg Brooks, Dougal Hutchison and their colleagues at the National Foundation for Educational Research for bringing their expertise to the evaluation of this programme.

We are grateful to them for providing initial advice in constructing the scope and terms of the evaluation, for their statistical analysis and interpretation of the data and their ongoing advice on integrating the qualitative analysis from the fieldwork into the overall evaluation.

The full description of the statistical analysis of the evaluation data by NFER is in Appendix 1.

The Basic Skills Agency would also like to thank all the Family Numeracy co-ordinators, teachers, tutors, advisers, inspectors, parents and children who took part in the pilot programme. We are grateful to them for their commitment to the programme.

A full list of the funded partnerships is in Appendix 3.

© The Basic Skills Agency
Commonwealth House, 1-19 New Oxford Street, London WC1A 1NU.

All rights reserved. No part of this publication may be photocopied, recorded or otherwise reproduced, stored in a retrieval system or transmitted in any form or by any electronic or mechanical means without the prior permission of the copyright owner.

Published October 1998

ISBN 1 85990 083 6

Design: Studio 21

Contents

Appendices

Dr Greg Brooks and Dougal Hutchison

- A full description of the statistical analysis of the evaluation data
- Quantitative data collection instruments
- Control group issues
- Qualitative data collection instruments

Foreword

WE know that poor numeracy skills have a major impact on how well people do as adults. This is particularly so in the world of work, where getting and keeping a job and promotion are more difficult for someone with poor numeracy.

So it's worrying that so many children, young people and adults in the UK struggle with poor numeracy skills; most surveys and research suggest that rather more struggle here than in many of our main competitor countries. This is all a little depressing but there are grounds for some optimism that we can change our present woeful position.

The new National Numeracy Strategy will do a great deal to improve standards in schools and make sure that children develop sound mathematical skills before they enter the adult world. And Family Numeracy – as this report illustrates – is a new initiative that works.

Family Numeracy, like family literacy, helps parents to improve their own numeracy skills, helps them help their children with numeracy and gives an immediate boost to children at risk of failing in numeracy.

We encouraged a range of experimental approaches in the fourteen pilot Family Numeracy programmes we funded. This Report produced by the Agency and NFER describes how effective these programmes were. Read the report for the detailed information but, in brief, both the parents and the children had made considerable progress in improving numeracy through these programmes. And the children who took part made far greater gains than their peer group not on the programme.

The report also describes the characteristics of the most effective practice and includes information on what has worked best in the recruitment and retention of the families, planning of the curriculum and teaching approach. I hope it will help anyone wanting to set up a Family Numeracy programme.

Alan Wells,
Director,
The Basic Skills Agency

Executive Summary

What is Family Numeracy?

THE BASIC SKILLS AGENCY piloted the Family Numeracy programme between April 1997 and March 1998. We wanted to find out if an intergenerational numeracy programme, for both parents and their children, could work as effectively as the Family Literacy programme. Family Numeracy aims to help break the cycle of underachievement and low expectation in numeracy in families where the parents themselves have poor numeracy.

The aim of the pilot programme was to investigate the most effective methods of:

- *raising the level of home support for numeracy;*

- *offering a quick-start and immediate gains in numeracy for 3-5 year old children at risk of underattainment;*

- *offering a re-start for their parents' numeracy learning and an impact on their numeracy level.*

All the pilot programmes were based in areas of disadvantage. They were run in primary schools, nursery schools, family centres, playgroups and a range of other locations where the number of children receiving free school meals was higher than the local and, in most cases, the national average. The schools who took part all had lower attainment in mathematics at the end of Key Stages 1 and 2 than the national average.

The programmes offered intensive provision to parents who have few, if any, qualifications and to their children, aged 3-5. The pilots were encouraged to experiment and therefore the number of hours offered varied ranging between 20 to 75 hours for each participant; courses lasted no more than 12 weeks. Most offered three strands of provision within a course or series of workshops. They therefore included separate sessions for the parents and children to work on developing their numeracy and joint sessions for the parents and children to work together. The joint sessions focused on practical ways parents could support early numeracy learning at home. The teaching was delivered by teachers/tutors qualified in teaching Early Years/Adult Basic Skills. The pilots were designed to link to the pre-school/school curriculum, existing home-school arrangements for mathematics and, where relevant at that time, the National Numeracy Project.

A framework for the evaluation of the pilot programme was established by the Agency with the National Foundation for Educational Research (NFER).

Did the Pilot Programmes Work?

- *The children who took part in the Family Numeracy pilot programme made statistically significantly more progress than the children in the control group.*

- *The children's progress in both number and mathematical language was statistically significant.*

- *Compared to the control group, 19% more children in the Family Numeracy group are now in the higher band of attainment having achieved on 6 or more items of the (SCAA/QCA) baseline scales.*

- *In comparison to their control group, 10% more Family Numeracy children (23% of the total Family Numeracy group) were able to show competence against all items of the Baseline Assessment scales by the end of the course.*

- *The pilot programme was judged to be equally successful for boys and girls and for monolingual and bilingual children.*

- *There was a statistically significant increase in a wide range of numeracy related activities at home during the course.*

- *Parents increased their contact with their child's class teacher by the end of the course and were more involved with school activities and supporting in class.*

- *84% of parents gained at least one unit of accreditation in Numberpower or similar accreditation in those programmes that gave the opportunity to do so.*

What Kind of Programme Works Best?

The most effective courses offered provision to meet each of the three aims. Where one of these elements was missing or lacked focus the gains in the other two target areas were less. Programmes which offered a structured adult numeracy curriculum in addition to separate sessions for the children and joint sessions for the parents and children led to:

- *the highest rates of accreditation for the parents;*

- *the highest rates of progress for the children;*

- *the highest rates of progress in supporting at home.*

After an identified number of hours (40 to 45 hours) the relative increase in gains for the children appear to diminish. Double the hours in one week did not appear to lead to double the gains.

The evaluation of the results from the different pilot programmes has enabled us to identify the core features that should be in place for a Family Numeracy programme to work most successfully for both the children and the adults.

Core features of a successful model

Three strands of provision with joint and separate sessions for both adults and children that offer:

- *a minimum of 1 hour weekly of joint sessions;*

- *a minimum of 2 hours weekly of separate sessions for the parents – split to allow adequate time to improve their own numeracy and to develop their ability to support their children at home;*

- *a minimum of 1½ hours weekly for the children which can be split into 2 sessions of 45 minutes;*

- *minimum of 40-45 hours;*

- *the same ratio of hours if more hours are offered;*

- *joint and separate sessions sequenced to ensure links and continuity;*

- *joint sessions jointly planned and staffed by Early Years and Adult Basic Skills teachers.*

A firmly structured numeracy curriculum that is:

- *applied rigorously;*

- *based on challenging numeracy obectives for each strand;*

- *focused on progress in a selected and achievable range of numeracy skills and concepts;*

- *planned with meaningful and explicit links between the different strands of provision;*

- *drawn from the Desirable Outcomes for Learning or the Early Years content of the National Framework for Mathematics and the National Curriculum for mathematics for the children and joint sessions;*

- *leading to accreditation of numeracy gains for the adults (and optionally of their learning in how to support their children's numeracy).*

Teaching in the children's sessions which focuses on:

- *modelling target numeracy concepts and skills in the introductory part of the session;*

- *acquiring mathematical language and number concepts through practical activities;*

- *using questioning techniques to extend dialogue about the maths involved in an activity and begin to develop mental fluency with number.*

Teaching in the joint sessions which focuses on:

- *modelling of approaches used by teachers in the children's sessions, for example, the use of play scenarios and games, drawing out new mathematical language, extending or confirming understanding through questioning;*

- *building in opportunities for the parents to use what they have seen immediately and therefore be practically engaged;*

- *making links between the activities and home contexts so that they are immediately transferable.*

A 'bridging' activity to be used at home each week which is introduced to both parents and children and helps to establish home routines.

Teaching in the adult sessions which focuses on:

- *whole group objectives for improving numeracy;*

- *an introductory session which focuses on the target numeracy in a 'real world' context and examines as a group the underpinning skills and strategies needed;*

- *opportunities to practice underpinning skills and strategies and apply them to authentic tasks;*

- *opportunities to reflect on and prepare for the joint sessions and home support of numeracy.*

Each kind of session has:

- *a challenging pace;*

- *maximum time spent on task for all participants;*

- *a focus on the maths involved not on the procedures involved in, for example, making number games.*

There was also a variety of 'supplementary' features that characterised the different pilot programmes. These additional features allowed the programmes to adapt to particular local circumstances. In many cases they increased the capacity of the programme to attract harder to reach groups of parents and their children. These included:

- *the use of vocational contexts for the adults' learning;*

- *the use of existing home visiting arrangements as an initial taster for the parents of younger children who would be least likely to join a course without support;*

- *the use of health visitors for supported self-referral;*

- *the use of bi-lingual teachers and assistants;*

- *the use of community outreach workers.*

1. Introduction

THE Basic Skills Agency piloted the Family Numeracy programme between April 1997 and March 1998. We wanted to find out if an intergenerational numeracy programme, aimed at both parents[1] and their children, could work as effectively as the Family Literacy programme.

14 partnerships successfully bid to develop a Family Numeracy initiative within the pilot programme in England. Local Education Authorities led eleven of the partnerships, a further two were jointly managed by the LEA and the local Further Education College and one partnership was co-ordinated by the Voluntary Services Policy Unit of a local council. Three of the participating LEAs were also part of the National Numeracy Project and another was an associate member.

All the courses and workshops were run in areas of disadvantage. There was also evidence of children's underattainment compared to the national average in maths at the end of Key Stage 1 and 2 in these areas.

Over 500 families took part in the pilot programme. A total of 62 courses or workshop programmes were run.

The Family Numeracy pilot programme included a variety of locally designed approaches. Almost all the courses (59) were aimed at parents with children between 3 and 5 years old. Some courses included children who were 2 years old and one workshop programme was aimed at children between 5 and 10 years old.

The aim was to investigate the most effective methods of:

- *providing greater home support for numeracy;*

- *offering a quick-start into numeracy for pre-school and Reception children at risk of underattainment;*

- *offering a re-start for their parents' numeracy learning.*

The Family Numeracy programme did **not** aim to:

▶ provide an early form of additional numeracy support for the children alone;

▶ offer only separate school or pre-school based adult education provision for the adults;

▶ offer solely information and explanation to parents about how maths is taught at school.

---

1. We use the term parent to include anyone who has the primary responsibility for the care of the child.

2. Why Family Numeracy?

FAMILY NUMERACY aims to help break the cycle of underachievement and low expectation in numeracy that affects the lives of some families. It offers provision to parents who have few if any qualifications and helps prevent the early failure of children in the same family.

We know when parents have poor basic skills, including poor numeracy, their children are more likely to experience the same difficulties.[2] Similarly, parents improving their own skills on 'stand-alone' adult basic skills programmes will not automatically impact upon their children's learning. A programme that also includes the opportunity for parents to learn ways of supporting their children's numeracy at home has the potential to offer double value to the family and economy.

Family Numeracy appears in the context of the emergent National Numeracy Strategy and is intended to complement the schools work by providing programmes for parents and children particularly where educational underattainment is common. The programme sought to build on established initiatives promoting parental support for numeracy development such as IMPACT. This and similar systems are already a familiar part of the landscape of home-school links in many schools.

---

2. *Parents and Their Children: The Intergenerational Effects of Poor Basic Skills,* ALBSU.

We know that progress for both the children and adults on the Family Literacy programme is immediate and continues after the courses.[3] The programme has had considerable success in attracting adults with literacy needs back into improving their own ability to read and write. We wanted to find out if a Family Numeracy programme could have the same effect.

The impact of poor numeracy

People with poor numeracy skills are more likely to be unemployed for longer periods than people with better numeracy.[4] Research also shows that poor numeracy represents a bigger problem for staying in full time employment than poor literacy.[5] Those with low level numeracy skills who are in employment are more likely to have a lower income, have less chance of on the job training and have less chance of promotion. They will have a more limited range of jobs to choose from. Adults with poor

literacy and numeracy struggle to fulfil their responsibilities as parents, citizens and consumers and are at greater risk of social exclusion.

Yet, as a culture, we continue to believe that it doesn't really matter if we have fewer numeracy skills than we might. There is less stigma attached to poor numeracy but also less importance. The impact of poor numeracy on life chances is perhaps less well known.

We tend to believe that the impact on everyday life of poor numeracy outside the workplace is not that great – we get by. Yet the growing responsibility we all have to take for handling our own money affairs means that those with

3. *Family Literacy Lasts: The NFER follow-up study of the Basic Skills Agency Demonstration Programmes,* Greg Brooks et al, 1997.
4. *It doesn't get any better: The impact of poor basic skills on the lives of 37 year olds,* John Bynner and Samantha Parsons, Basic Skills Agency, 1997.
5. *Does Numeracy Matter?* John Bynner and Samantha Parsons, Basic Skills Agency, 1997.

poor numeracy are increasingly at risk of marginalisation. Making sure we get what we are entitled to, dealing with credit, loans or down payments, sorting out insurance and pensions require better numeracy. These kinds of ordinary transactions increasingly involve more than being able to perform simple calculations. We need to be able to interpret complex graphical and statistical information, work out percentages as a matter of course, understand financial projections and so on.

The scale of the problem

22% of adults in England and Wales have very low numeracy.[6] Similar figures emerged from the International Adult Literacy Survey which assessed competence in quantitative literacy.[7] This is defined as the 'knowledge and skills required to apply arithmetic operations to numbers embedded in printed materials'.

This figure of 22% of course disguises significant regional differences with higher concentrations of people with low numeracy in some areas. Comparisons with other similar industrialised countries show that standards of basic numeracy are generally poorer in England both among children and adults.[8] A similar picture exists for adults in Wales.

There are more people with poor numeracy in poorer households. The *International Numeracy Survey* showed that there is a significant difference between the numeracy levels in white-collar households (ABC1s) and working class households (C2DEs). The same survey found that the group of adults between 16-34 years old struggled most with basic numeracy.

The gap in the level of numeracy attainment between boys and girls during school has been reducing for some time. Women who left school some time ago are still less proficient. 27% of women compared to 19% of men were found to have poor numeracy in the *Does Numeracy Matter?* study.[9] Couple this with the growing demand by employers for numeracy skills in the kinds of jobs women traditionally seek, such as clerical/secretarial jobs, then the need to close the numeracy gap and raise the level of numeracy skills of both men and women takes on added urgency.[10]

6. *Does Numeracy Matter?* Bynner and Parsons, Basic Skills Agency, 1997
7. *Adult Literacy in Britain,* Carey, Low, Hansbro, The Stationery Office, 1997
8. *International Numeracy Survey,* Basic Skills Agency, 1997; *Third International Mathematics and Science Study, Third National Report,* Harris, Keys, Fernandes, NFER, 1997

Improving adults' numeracy

Attracting adults back into education to improve their numeracy skills has never been easy. There was an 18% increase in the number of adults in numeracy programmes in 1995/6. This represents just over 44,000 adults receiving help with numeracy and a further c.88,000 receiving help for both literacy and numeracy combined.

If we compare this to the 22% of the population who do not have adequate functional competence in numeracy, the need to develop other effective ways of delivering numeracy provision becomes clear.

Improving children's attainment

The national 2002 target of 75% of 11 year olds achieving Level 4 in mathematics, the work of the Numeracy Taskforce and the National Numeracy Strategy in England have all given a focus and rigour to the drive to improve numeracy standards. In Wales the target is that 60% – 70% should achieve Level 4 by 2000, and rising to 70% – 80% by the year 2002.

The Family Numeracy Programme is intended to complement the government's strategy to raise standards in schools by:

- *offering opportunities for parents and young children, who most need it, to improve their numeracy skills;*

- *enabling parents to provide a background of support for numeracy at home and see the potential that ordinary activities and play can offer for hands on and mental maths experience;*

- *informing parents about what and how their children are learning at nursery or school and giving them practical and appropriate ways to translate this to everyday life at home;*

- *forming a bridge between school and 'real world' maths for children most at risk of underattainment in maths;*

- *offering parents the chance to influence their children's attitude and aspirations in maths;*

- *involving the local community in recognising the importance of raising numeracy skills for its regeneration.*

9. *Does Numeracy Matter?* Bynner and Parsons, Basic Skills Agency, 1997
10. *Does Numeracy Matter?* Bynner and Parsons, Basic Skills Agency, 1997

3. The Family Numeracy pilot evaluation

OST provision was delivered between September 1997 and March 1998 allowing initial time for planning, staff development and recruitment.

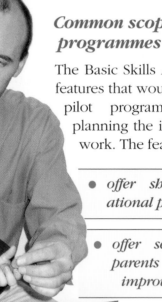

Common scope of the programmes

The Basic Skills Agency set out a number of features that would be important for the local pilot programmes to consider when planning the innovatory Family Numeracy work. The features were, to:

- *offer short intensive intergenerational provision;*

- *offer separate sessions for the parents and children to work on improving their numeracy;*

- *offer joint sessions for the parents and children focusing on practical ways parents can support early numeracy learning at home;*

- *recruit parents whose numeracy was below Level 1 of the Basic Skills Agency Standards (this corresponds broadly to less than GCSE in mathematics) and with few if any formal qualifications;*

- *staff courses with teachers/tutors qualified in teaching Early Years and Adult Basic Skills;*

- *offer opportunities for parents to embark on nationally recognised accreditation, such as Numberpower if they wished to do so;*

- *offer creche support;*

- *make links with the pre-school/school curriculum, existing home-school arrangements for mathematics and, where relevant at that time, with the National Numeracy Project;*

- *set target outcomes for progress, recruitment, attendance and retention.*

Other features the programmes had in common

All the programmes had a number of essential features without which they would not have been able to deliver the provision.

Features that made attendance possible

The pilot programmes:

▶ ran courses in places (schools, nurseries, family centres etc.) which were familiar to the parents and easily accessible;

▶ planned a recruitment strategy which included measures to motivate those parents most likely to benefit and least likely to come forward;

▶ used the class teachers' and headteachers' knowledge of the children and parents most likely to benefit to identify the families;

▶ produced simple and clear publicity material which was easy to read;

▶ conducted individual interviews with the parents;

▶ provided ongoing support and motivation to stay on the programme;

▶ provided accommodation for both parents' and children's sessions.

Setting up the partnerships

The pilot programmes:

▶ ensured adequate matched funding from the LEA (and in some cases a range of other partners including FEFC, SRB, TEC, EBP, Social Services, trusts);

▶ ensured the partnership offered a range of expertise and experience;

▶ ensured that lead, advice, monitoring and delivery roles were clear;

▶ ensured local support from the headteacher or head of centre.

Evaluation framework

A framework for the evaluation of the pilot programme was established with the National Foundation for Educational Research (NFER). Each of the 14 pilot programmes provided the Agency and NFER with common data.

The evaluation was based on information on:

● *the numbers of parents and children taking part and their educational and linguistic background;*

● *the assessed progress in the participating children's numeracy competence from the beginning to the end of the course (this was possible only for those children between 4 and 5.3 years old at the start of the course);*

● *the progress during the same period (using the same assessment procedure) of a control group of children in each LEA with the closest match for age, experience and background possible;*

- *changes in how often numeracy-focused home activity took place and changes in the kind of activity;*

- *how many families were recruited to each course, how many remained and how often they attended;*

- *how many adults gained full or partial accreditation of their numeracy gains;*

- *other areas of progress and progression.*

The children were assessed using:

▶ the two mathematical scales of the SCAA (now QCA) Baseline Assessment;
▶ the SCAA procedure for administering the assessment.

The two scales measured the children's competence at the beginning and end of the intervention in:

▶ using and understanding number;
▶ using and understanding mathematical language.

The adults' progress was assessed using a variety of means depending on the nature of the local initiative.

The full set of templates used for the evaluation is in Appendix 2. The Basic Skills Agency conducted the fieldwork for the evaluation. NFER conducted the statistical analysis of the data.

4. Who took part in the pilot programmes?

ALL the schools selected by the LEAs demonstrated a high level of need. The children were attaining below the national average at KS1 and/or KS2 in mathematics. Large numbers of children attending the schools were in receipt of free school meals. The majority of the schools were above their LEA and national averages in this respect. The majority of the pilots were in areas where the benchmark survey of adult basic skills levels shows a high percentage of people with very low numeracy.[11]

517 parents and 515 children took part in the Family Numeracy pilot programme.

The programme reached women almost exclusively; 499 of the adults taking part were female.

English was an additional language for 12% of the parents.

69% of the adults taking part were aged 16 to 34.

Of the children who took part 58% were boys and 42% girls.

The parents who took part were generally:

- **poorly qualified;**
  56% of the parents had no qualifications. Very few of the parents had post-16 qualifications in mathematics (7%).
  Just 38 parents reported they had previously had any basic skills tuition.

- **not employed outside the home.**
  75% of the parents reported that they were either unemployed or looking after the family.

Retention on the Family Numeracy courses was high.
84% of the parents who enrolled stayed on the courses until they ended .

11. Adults' Basic Skills CD ROM, Basic Skills Agency, 1998

5. Progress made on the pilot programmes

THE full description of the statistical analysis from the evaluation data by NFER and their detailed report on the progress made by the participants, are in Appendix 1.

Summary of the children's progress[12]

The children who took part in the Family Numeracy pilot programme made **statistically significantly more progress than the children in the control group.** The effect size, representing the relative amount of progress, was judged by NFER to be good for the length of the intervention.

> ▶ The children's progress on both the number scale and the mathematical language scale was statistically significant.

This means that overall the children who took part in the Family Numeracy programme made considerable progress in both number and mathematical language.

The pilot programme was judged to be equally successful for boys and girls and for monolingual and bilingual children.

---

12. Some of the children who took part in the programme were 3 years old at the start of the course. The assessment procedure was not valid for this age group. The summary of gains reflects the progress made by the children who were 4 years or older at the start of the Family Numeracy courses.

In comparison with their peers in similar circumstances, whose gains were due to maturation and their usual learning in school, **the Family Numeracy children are now ahead in their acquisition of early numeracy competence. They are better placed in the terms of the Desirable Outcomes for Learning at the end of Nursery to take up the National Curriculum for Mathematics. They have achieved a higher baseline than their peers.**

Most significant comparative progress was seen for the Family Numeracy children on the later items of both the number and mathematical language scales which tested higher level competencies.

	Family Numeracy children		Control Group children	
	beginning %	end %	beginning %	end %
Number				
Aware of addition	40	71	35	53
Solves problems	14	42	11	19
Mathematical language				
Numbers to 10	21	56	26	38
Explains addition	10	29	10	19

The graph below shows that there is a clear difference in the baseline profile of the two groups by the end of the course. 22% of children in the control group compared to 11% of the Family Numeracy group remain in the lowest band having achieved on 2 or fewer items of the number and mathematical language scales together. 40% of children in the control group remain in the middle band achieving on 3 to 5 items of the two scales compared to 30% of the Family Numeracy children.

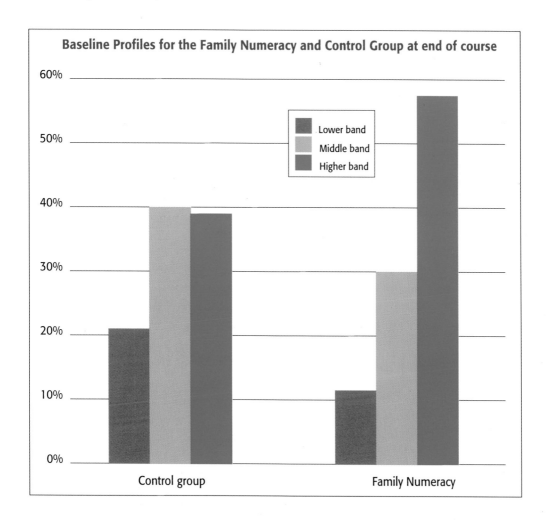

Compared to the control group, **19% more children in the Family Numeracy group are now in the higher band of attainment having achieved on 6 or more items of the baseline scales.** By the end of the intervention, 57% of Family Numeracy children were in this higher band compared to 38% of the control group children. Before the intervention roughly equal numbers of children in the Family Numeracy group (21%) and the control group (23%) were in this band with the majority of these children in both groups at the lower reaches of the band.

Compared to the control group again, 10% more children in the Family Numeracy group (23% versus 13%) were able to show competence against **all** items of the Baseline Assessment scales by the end of the course.

No data is currently available nationally to establish the children's relative baseline or end of course position against national norms.

Nevertheless taking account of:

- *the fact that the children were from areas of multiple disadvantage;*

- *the fact that the children were from areas where attainment in numeracy is below the national average;*

- *the comparison with the control group data;*

- *the increases in the frequency and range of home activity;*

the Family Numeracy children's progress was:

> ▶ above the average of their non-participating peers in like circumstances;
> ▶ attributable to the intervention;
> ▶ attributable to the additional input from both teachers and parents.

Progress

Results for the children who were younger than 4 years old at the start of their course were not possible using the assessment procedure established by NFER and the Agency. Programmes which only worked with 3 to 4 year olds established and analysed their own assessments. These results suggest a similar picture of achievement and progress.

Summary of other progress for the children

Early Years teachers were also asked to report from their ongoing assessments on other areas of gains that they had observed in the Family Numeracy children. All the areas were selected because they were not tested by the SCAA mathematical scales and were skills and attitudes critical to numeracy development and for access to other areas of the curriculum.

● *90% of the Family Numeracy children had increased their interest in using toys, games, books and taking part in roleplay involving numbers and maths.*

● *88% of the Family Numeracy children had increased their confidence in dealing with numerical situations.*

● *76% of the Family Numeracy children had improved their understanding of instructions and questions relating to calculating, making decisions and estimating.*

● *98% of the Family Numeracy children had gained in confidence.*

● *88% of the Family Numeracy children had improved their concentration and perseverance and had a greater eagerness to explore and initiate new learning.*

● *70% of the Family Numeracy children had improved their speaking and listening skills overall.*

The cause and effect of development in these areas of attitude and motivation is always difficult to determine precisely. We cannot therefore be definite about attributing these gains to the effect of the Family Numeracy programme and not to normal maturation.

Summary of the parents' progress in supporting their children's numeracy development

Family Numeracy acknowledges the fact that parents play a major role as their children's first educators. One of the three aims of the programme is to enhance the capacity of parents to provide early and ongoing support for their children's numeracy at home.

As part of the evaluation we collected information on the kind of activities parents were already doing with their children at home at the start of the courses. We measured the changes in how often a whole range of numeracy focused activities took place by the end of the course. Were the parents stimulated by what they had learnt on the courses to try out a wider range of home based activity? Did these activities become part of the home routines? Did the parents who did not have the confidence to attempt any activity involving their children in numeracy at home begin to do so?

The full set of data showing the changes in how often parents and children took part in numeracy related home activities was collected using the Home Activities Questionnaire which is in Appendix 2. Course tutors and teachers worked with parents at the beginning and end of the courses to complete the questionnaire.

All the numeracy-related home activities showed an increase by the end of the course. The increase was statistically significant in every case but one. The exception was *'Does your child play with construction kits/building blocks with you?'* – this was already very frequent at the beginning of the course.

When 'frequent' is considered to be once a week or more, the greatest increases by the end of the courses were seen in the activities listed opposite.

The items in this list were among the kinds of activities parents and children were taking part in, in joint sessions.

The general picture was that a wide range of numeracy related home activities increased during the course and became firmly embedded in family practice.

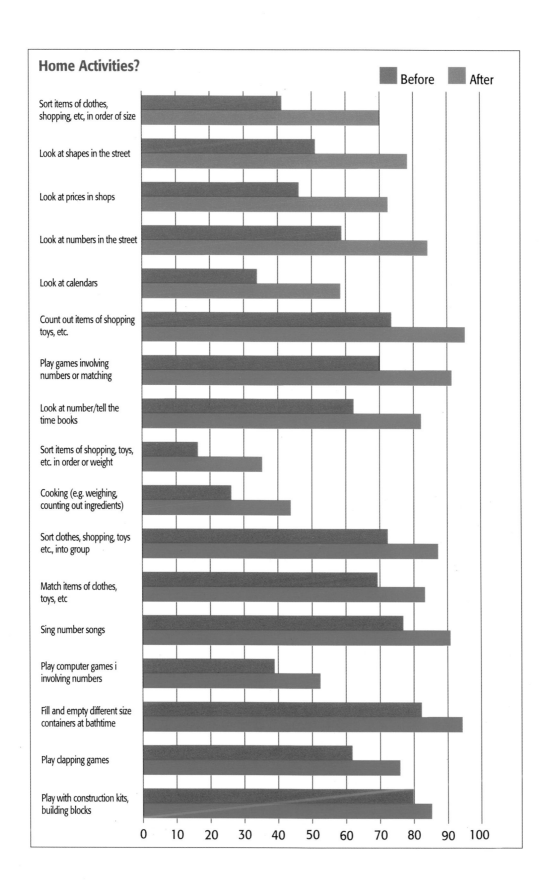

Home Activities?

Legend: Before, After

- Sort items of clothes, shopping, etc, in order of size
- Look at shapes in the street
- Look at prices in shops
- Look at numbers in the street
- Look at calendars
- Count out items of shopping toys, etc.
- Play games involving numbers or matching
- Look at number/tell the time books
- Sort items of shopping, toys, etc. in order or weight
- Cooking (e.g. weighing, counting out ingredients)
- Sort clothes, shopping, toys etc., into group
- Match items of clothes, toys, etc
- Sing number songs
- Play computer games i involving numbers
- Fill and empty different size containers at bathtime
- Play clapping games
- Play with construction kits, building blocks

Scale: 0 10 20 30 40 50 60 70 80 90 100

Summary of the changing relationship with the school

Parents were asked to report at the beginning and end of the courses on their contact with their children's school.

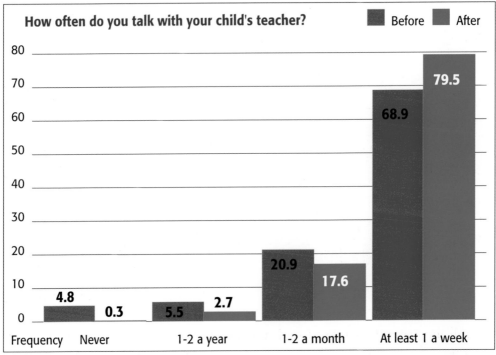

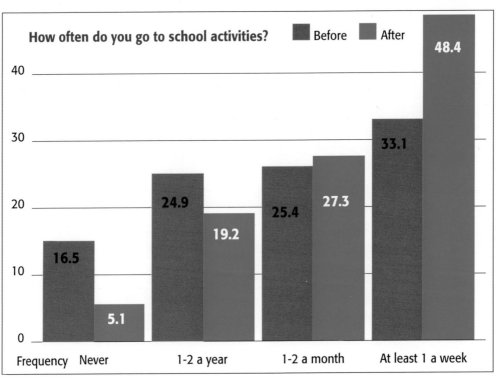

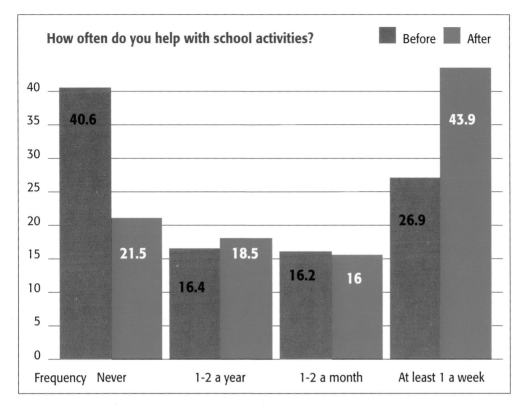

How often do you help with school activities?

Before After

Frequency	Never	1-2 a year	1-2 a month	At least 1 a week
Before	40.6	16.4	16.2	26.9
After	21.5	18.5	16	43.9

Overall the parents increased their contact with their child's class teacher by the end of the course. They were more involved with school activities, attending and helping with classes and trips.

Summary of the parents' progress in numeracy

The picture of the progress in the adult's numeracy is less precisely known because:

- *local programmes used their own initial and ongoing assessment and the information therefore was reported as tutor assessment. Examples of initial assessment procedures used, included the Basic Skills Agency Initial Assessment, Numberpower tasks and AEB initial assessments;*

- *some programmes used short courses as stepping stones and only had time to achieve partial completion of units through Numberpower;*

- *some programmes intended to use accreditation in follow up provision as a form of final assessment and information on the rate of accreditation from these subsequent courses was therefore not yet available.*

Nevertheless the longer courses and more effective shorter courses that set rates of accreditation as target outcomes, achieved or exceeded their targets.

We can see that where adult provision, even when quite short, was of high quality and set high expectations, rates of accreditation were high.

The rate of accreditation overall in those programmes in which it was a feature was 84% of parents gaining at least one unit of accreditation in Numberpower or similar.

9 of the 14 pilots offered parents the opportunity to accredit their numeracy by the end of the course. Accreditation in these cases was a voluntary option.

Where there was between 15 and 25 hours of dedicated adult numeracy provision and where there was the opportunity to take accreditation, the accreditation rates were between 67% and 100% accreditation of at least 1 unit of Numberpower or like accreditation.

Some of the pilot programmes did not feature provision for the adults' own numeracy development from the beginning of the course believing that this would deter participation. They designed the three-strand programme so that the adults would embark on their own numeracy curriculum towards the end of the course. In most cases this was jointly funded with FEFC and continued after the other two strands of provision had finished.

The evidence suggests that where there was sufficient guidance about the benefits of progression, and timely introduction to the adult basic skills tutors, take up of this strand of the provision was reasonable.

However, more importantly, there is evidence to suggest that when the programmes' three aims were made clear to parents from the beginning and presented positively within a climate of high expectation, this did not present a deterrent to recruitment or retention. The expectation that improvements in their own numeracy would indeed support their children's learning in mathematics was well founded.

6. What works best?
A model of effective Family Numeracy provision

THE 14 pilot programmes offered a variety of provision within the guidelines of the overall programme. The Agency was looking for some innovation and experimentation in the characteristics of the different programmes in order to find out what worked best.

The pilots varied in the way they combined certain features. Some offered a greater numbers of hours for each strand while combining joint and separate sessions in various sequences and proportions. The pilots explored offering different contexts for learning and teaching approaches and gave different emphases to the curriculum. Most of the courses were run in primary or nursery schools though there was some use of other locations such as family centres and the workplace.

The data used as the basis for judgements on effectiveness was collected from:

- *the NFER statistical analysis of the assessment framework;*

- *the evaluative visits to the projects by the Basic Skills Agency;*

- *analysis of the final reports from the programme co-ordinators;*

- *analysis of teachers' and tutors' opinions;*

- *analysis of the components of the programmes where the parents and children made the greatest gains.*

The evaluation framework measures how successful the different programmes were in achieving progress in the triple aims of Family Numeracy. **Some features were critical to the effectiveness** of the programmes while the presence of **other features simply allowed a programme to adjust to local need** and give access to harder to reach target groups but did not impact on effectiveness per se. (For information on accessing harder to reach groups, see section 7).

This allows us to identify the combination of features that need to be in place for the core model to work most successfully and those supplementary features that can be modified to adapt the core model so that it is fit for local purpose.

Features of a core model of effective Family Numeracy provision

▶ **Three strands of provision** with joint and separate sessions for both adults and children that offer:

  – a minimum of **1 hour weekly of joint sessions;**

  – a minimum of **2 hours weekly of separate sessions for the parents** – split to allow adequate time to improve their own numeracy and to develop their ability to support their children at home;

  – a minimum of **1½ hours weekly for the children** – split, if appropriate, into 2 sessions of 45 minutes;

  – the **same ratio of hours if more hours are offered;**

  – a minimum of **40-45 hours;**

  – joint and separate sessions which are **sequenced in a way that ensures links** and continuity;

  – joint sessions **jointly planned and staffed** by Early Years and Adult Basic Skills experts.

▶ A firmly **structured numeracy curriculum** which is:

  – applied rigorously;

  – based on challenging numeracy objectives for each strand;

  – focused wholly on progress in a selected range of numeracy skills and concepts that is achievable in the time;

  – planned with meaningful and explicit **links between the different strands** of provision;

  – for the children **drawn from the Desirable Outcomes for Learning or the Early Years content of the National Framework for Mathematics and the National Curriculum for Mathematics;**

  – for the **adults leading to accreditation of their numeracy gains** (and optionally of their learning in how to support their children's numeracy).

► **Teaching in the children's sessions which focuses on:**

– *'modelling' target numeracy concepts and skills in the introductory part of the session;*

– *acquiring mathematical language and number concepts through practical activities;*

– *the use of questioning* techniques to:

- **extend dialogue** about the maths involved in an activity;

- begin to **develop mental fluency with number.**

► **Teaching in the joint sessions which focuses on:**

– *modelling of the approaches used by the teachers in the children's sessions* i.e. use of play scenarios and games, drawing out new mathematical language, extending or confirming understanding through questioning;

– **opportunities for the parents to use what they have seen** immediately and therefore be practically engaged with the activities and their children's work on them;

– links between the activities and **home contexts** so that they are immediately transferable;

– a 'bridging' activity to be used at home which is introduced to both parents and children.

> **Teaching in the adults' sessions which focuses on:**

  – *whole group objectives for improving numeracy and individual action plans;*

  – *an introductory session which focuses on the target numeracy in a 'real world' context, the context of developing children's numeracy and examines as a group the underpinning skills and strategies needed;*

  – *opportunities to practice underpinning skills and strategies and apply them to authentic tasks;*

  – *opportunities to reflect on and prepare for the joint sessions and home support of numeracy.*

  – *a challenging* **pace;**

  – *maximum* **time spent on task** *for all participants;*

  – *a* **focus on the maths involved not on the procedures** *involved in, for example, making number games;*

> *'Bridging' activities between sessions to be undertaken at home each week thereby establishing home routines.*

The main finding is that the most effective courses were made up of the features above and offered provision to meet each of the three aims. Where one of these elements was missing or lacked focus the gains in the other two target areas were less. For example, programmes which offered a firmly structured adult numeracy curriculum led to:

● *the highest rates of accreditation for the parents;*

● *the highest rates of progress for the children;*

● *the highest rates of progress in supporting at home.*

This suggests that the climate of expectation and confidence created in motivating the parents to improve their own skills supports involvement in activity that leads to progress for their children. It also suggests that there is a prevailing climate of aspiration and achievement created both in the family and in the course or programme.

A further finding is that after an identified number of hours (40 to 45 hours) the relative increase in gains for the children appears to diminish. **Double the hours in one week did not appear to double the gains.**

The most effective programmes made clear to the parents from the beginning that these were intensive courses. They maintained a quick pace and high expectation of achievement throughout the course. The response to this was that the majority of parents on these courses covered considerable ground on their own at home. They consolidated and applied what had been learnt in the session, both in their own numeracy and in their support for their children.

The less effective courses offered provision that incorporated more diffuse aims such as dealing with behaviour at home. They tended not to apply the numeracy curriculum in a consistent way. These joint and adult sessions were too often side-tracked into off-task general discussion between the parents. One of the most effective of the pilots planned to address this social aspect of the courses by having a working lunch, planned and budgeted by the parents; this meant that the other sessions were intensively and exclusively focused on mathematical tasks.

7. How the model can be adapted to different local circumstances

ABOVE and beyond the features of the core model there were a variety of 'supplementary' features that characterised the different pilot programmes. The presence of these additional features allowed the programmes to adapt to particular local circumstances. In many cases they increased the capacity of the programme to attract harder to reach groups of parents and their children. In analysing their situation the steering groups for the pilots identified the means of strengthening recruitment, retention and delivery.

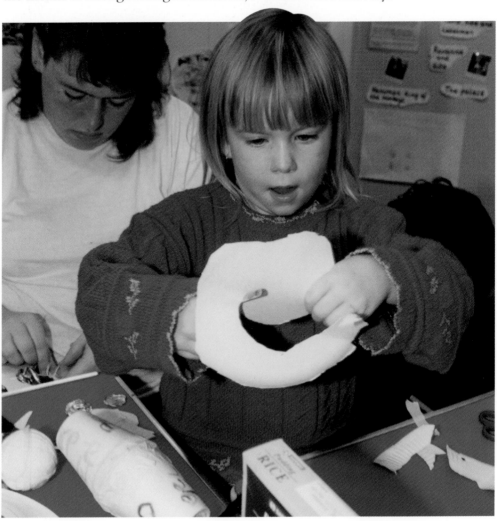

The 'map' below identifies, the ways in which the core model can be made fit for local purpose and the benefits and effects of the additional features.

Feature	Effect
Use of existing home visiting arrangements as first part of course, promoting 'numeracy play' in the visits	• Suitable for youngest children • Support for entry to group provision for least confident parents • Familiarisation with numeracy-focused activity in home • Initial inclusion of younger and older siblings and other family members • Support for women less likely to have contact beyond the home
Use of health visitors for supported self-referral to provision	• Reaches those least likely to come forward • Reaches those with younger children • Reaches those children who may not be in pre-school provision • Can target those younger adults who were early school leavers • Promotes introduction to education
Use of bi-lingual teachers/tutors or support assistants in sessions	• Supports numeracy learning • Supports inclusion of families for whom English is Additional Language
Use of community outreach workers	• Supports recruitment of those who have least contact with school • Supports retention via ongoing guidance on progression opportunities • Supports distance learning • Supports participation of groups at risk of social exclusion

Use of existing community facilities e.g. toy libraries, drop in family centre facilities, 'electronic village hall'	• Provides extended facilities for the courses • Provides motivation • Provides forum to continue activities after the 'course' • Reduces costs
Use of existing vocational contexts for learning e.g. curriculum construction centre at local F.E College, workplace	• Provides context for practical and relevant application of adults' numeracy learning • Provides opportunities for direct progression into further work related training • Adds to potential for attracting fathers into provision and into support for their children's learning
Use of school as course centre but drawing families not yet at the school who are within the catchment area	• Casts net wider to reach 'target' group • Provides an introduction to the school environment and school or nursery approach to numeracy
Use of EBP links	• Promotion of numeracy as workplace skill • Enables company speakers/visits and context for numeracy learning
Use of Saturday/evening provision	• Reaches more employed parents
Involvement of supermarkets and other retail outlets	• Enables visits and trails • Sponsorship • Contact with employers
Partnership with playgroups	• Delivers provision to younger children • Offers training opportunities to playgroup staff in early numeracy development
Partnership delivery with under 8's Social Services provision	• Reaches harder to reach families • Supports transition to mainstream nursery or school provision

8. Successful strategies – case studies and lessons

Recruitment

THE most successful recruitment ensured that the target group had been reached. In these cases all the adults were below Level 1 [of the Agency's Standards] in numeracy and had few if any qualifications. Their children were considered to be more likely to underattain in mathematics.

The pilots were asked to aim for a minimum of 10 families on each course. The most effective recruitment strategies reached this number and in some cases exceeded it, running courses for 11 and 12 families.

In some instances where recruitment was less successfully targeted, the presence of adults with better numeracy tended to distort the direction of the programme. It became more focused on solely finding out ways to support in the home and the classroom. Whilst informing and involving the wider group of parents is important, this was not the aim of the Family Numeracy pilot and so for our purposes is less effective.

Evidence suggests that a wider range of levels of numeracy (going above Level 1) among the parents within one course tends to deter those with numeracy needs from addressing them. This may be for fear of stigmatisation.

Most courses were aimed at children within a single 'year group': nursery or Reception. Some courses jointly provided, for example, by Social Services and Education, included a range of ages from 2 to 4 in one course.

We have identified, within the experience of the pilots, a number of strategies that when used together lead to the highest levels of recruitment from the target group.

Recruiting the target group in the right numbers is easier when:

▶ the programme has **the whole hearted and active support of the headteacher** or head of centre;

▶ simple attractive posters, flyers, notes or 'postcards' are produced that provide **clear initial information about the course** and/or any pre-course sessions. Readability is checked. Translation into other languages is available;

▶ at the same time or immediately following the publicity material **individual approaches are made to parents by the headteacher** or head of centre;

▶ pre-course tasters are planned by the steering group and practitioners;

▶ pre-course tasters are a 'window' into what the course will be like **in that:**

  – they are jointly led by the early years teacher and adult tutor;
  – they are 'hands-on' and allow parents to briefly sample the kind of joint activities and learning that will be offered;
  – the children are present for part of the time and take part in the activities;
  – they give clear information about the aims of the course and the target outcomes;
  – they ensure some time for individual discussion with parents;

- ▶ *pre-course tasters are held at times when parents are most likely to want to attend e.g. at drop off or collection times at nursery, school etc.;*

- ▶ *pre-course sessions take place away from the classroom and in a 'known' area of the school, nursery etc. for example the parents' room or hall;*

- ▶ **bi-lingual support or interpretation is on offer** *in the pre-course taster where it is likely to be needed;*

- ▶ *'enrolment' takes place during the pre-course sessions as far as possible;*

- ▶ *existing relevant* **community liaison services:** *voluntary and community groups (home-school liaison workers, community outreach workers, residents' associations, unemployed/refugee/women's groups etc.)* **are involved to publicise the course and support self-referral;**

- ▶ **participants from previous Family Numeracy courses are asked to support the 'marketing' of subsequent courses** *by 'passing the word' and speaking at pre-course sessions;*

- ▶ **experience and lessons from previous recruitment** *to other courses and activities* **in the same location is drawn on;**

- ▶ *there is a whole school view of parental partnership.*

Most of the pilots offered a carousel of simple games and tasks for the pre-course tasters which the parents could try out with their children supported by the course staff.

The pilot in *Lancashire LEA* used a consistent approach across its pilot schools for their taster sessions. The steering and planning group designed the framework for a family maths trail for the sessions. This included guidance to the schools on how to organise the event and involve parents.

Two of the pilots, Sefton LEA and Bulwell Vision partnership in Nottingham, successfully used existing home visiting arrangements to engage parents who would be least ready to join a course. They involved the parents and children at home in numeracy-focused play and games that the course would use. These parents then had the 'taster' session at home. An invitation and encouragement to join the course was given.

Retention

Overall, retention on the courses, after enrolment, was high at 84% and attendance similarly so at 83%. The evidence from the pilot programmes shows that **parents are most likely to have high levels of commitment and stay on the courses when:**

> ▶ courses are firmly structured and target outcomes for individuals are negotiated at the beginning of the course; **parents know clearly what they are trying to achieve;**
>
> ▶ **valid national accreditation is on offer;**
>
> ▶ the expectation of full attendance is made clear right from the beginning and **parents do not get the impression that it is a drop-in facility;**
>
> ▶ it is made clear to parents that Family Numeracy is a family learning programme and that their **child's attendance is dependent on their attendance;**
>
> ▶ **courses contain sufficient variety of experience** including visits, a variety of classroom groupings and approaches – hands on application, discussion, skills practice;
>
> ▶ courses are timed so that they do not clash with religious observance periods;
>
> ▶ **the headteacher** or 'head of centre' **is actively involved** and spends some time in sessions and checking progress and satisfaction with the course;
>
> ▶ there is a support system offered by 'outreach' staff **for parents who are least confident about re-entering education.**
> Outreach:
>   – will telephone or offer home visits;
>   – can offer individual 'catch-up' or support when needed;
>
> ▶ **parents are clearly informed about progression routes** into further study or training, including input from careers guidance officers and college staff;
>
> ▶ **the social aspect of courses is recognised and catered for in time limited breaks**/lunches etc. and not allowed to permeate the sessions so that they lose focus.

Planning and monitoring

The most effective provision shows that planning needs to operate at two levels – co-ordination across the programme and between the adult tutor and early years teacher within each location. Where this works best, roles and responsibilities are clearly marked out from the beginning. Each partner knows what they have to deliver and what role they have in monitoring and developing the programme.

Planning, co-ordination and monitoring across the programme

The most effective pro-grammes established a steering group representing the range of partners. The head-teacher or head of centre from each location was on the steering group as well as a representative of the adult provider. A representative from the Advisory and Inspection Service most often led the steering group.

The first step in all the most effective programmes was to consult and gain commitment from the host schools, nurseries and family centres to take part in the programme. The implications and benefits of participation were made clear. Many of the pilots held an introductory workshop to the programme with presentations to schools and other centres who would meet the criteria of need. The aim was to elicit their interest and commitment. The least cost effective programmes spent time after the event persuading schools that had been 'signed up' to the programme on the basis of need alone that they wanted to take part.

The steering group considered the characteristics of the local need and identified any additional features the programmes would need to include to meet that need. (See section *How the model can be adapted for different circumstances*). They established the target outcomes for recruitment, retention, attendance, progress and accreditation and progression for each course.

The planning of the curriculum outline and the teaching approaches was co-ordinated by the steering group for the whole programme. It was not left to individual teachers and tutors in isolation to plan the basic direction and objectives of the curriculum or the teaching approach. Where this level of planning was the responsibility of the individuals, given all other pressures on time for school and college staff, manageability and quality became an issue.

Ongoing monitoring of quality and progress was provided by the maths and early years advisers and inspectors as well as the programme co-ordinator. Advice and support were delivered in the same way. Feedback to the practitioners and steering group resulted in adjustments when necessary.

In the less effective programmes the absence of genuine participation by one or more of the partners had identifiable negative consequences as a result. In some cases poorer recruitment and retention than the programme had aimed for was due to the lack of sufficient liaison with community groups or headteachers. In other instances the lack of involvement of the local FE college or adult basic skills service from the planning stage reduced the likelihood of progress for the adults in improving their own numeracy or going onto further study or training if they so chose.

Planning and co-ordination between the adult tutor and early years teacher within one course

The partnership between the adult tutor and early years teacher is fundamental to the success of the course. The partnership needs to be supported by ensuring time for joint planning and review of joint sessions each week. This planning draws from the overall curriculum map. Where the planning for this session was done only by the early years teacher this affected the role and impact of the adult tutor in the session and the quality of the learning. In these cases the adults' sessions were more prone to be a bolt-on rather than an integral part of the programme. The preparation for parents to go into the joint sessions was minimal and generally consisted of discussion and explanation of developmental issues in numeracy.

In the most effective programmes the teacher and tutor also had sight of each other's planning for the separate sessions. The teacher and tutor collaborated not just on planning the content but also on developing common teaching methodologies. When, for instance, parents were asked to share and consider their own strategies for mental calculation, they understood more readily the ways of developing mental fluency which they saw the early years teacher using in the joint sessions.

Many programmes found it useful for the early years teacher to visit at least one session of adult provision early on and for the adult tutor to visit a children's session. In this way they had a clearer idea of how each other's practice could inform the planning and how it could be linked in appropriate ways to improve learning.

All planning in the most effective programmes was based on clear and detailed understanding of the starting points of individual children and adults on the course and regular review of their progress.

Staffing and training

For Family Numeracy to work at its most effective it is critical that all the partners and practitioners under-stand the aims of the programme and how they can be met.

The aims of the programme are:

- *to raise the level of home support for numeracy;*

- *to offer a quick-start and immediate gains in numeracy for 3-5 year old children at risk of underattainment;*

- *to offer a re-start for their parents' numeracy learning and raise their numeracy level.*

For the practitioners this involves understanding the nature of its three strands and how best to implement them.

Training and staff development can play a key role in making this happen. Training needs to embrace all the practitioners who will be involved in delivering the courses including the early years, adult tutors and any support staff. Some of the pilot programmes reported that almost all the difficulties they encountered could be traced back to lack of pre-course training.

Evidence from the most effective Family Numeracy pilots suggests that staff development prior to the course should include:

▶ *an initial INSET day or session/s;*

▶ *input from the maths and early years advisers and inspectors;*

▶ *input from the adult basic skills co-ordinator;*

▶ *a focus on understanding the aims of the programme;*

▶ *a focus on the objectives of the early years numeracy curriculum and those selected for the programme;*

▶ *a focus on the range of teaching contexts and approaches to be used e.g. imaginative play, games, problem solving and how these will be 'modelled' for the parents;*

▶ *a focus on the acquisition of mathematical language in developing numeracy;*

▶ *a focus on negotiating Individual Action Plans for the adults within the overall scheme of work;*

▶ *training in managing accreditation;*

▶ *training in the administration of the assessment instruments to be used for children and adults;*

▶ *a focus on involving parents and preparing for and managing the joint sessions;*

▶ *a focus on the role of home activities and ways of promoting these;*

▶ *training on recruiting the target group.*

For many practitioners, both early years teachers and adult tutors, some of the skills involved in implementing a Family Numeracy programme will be untried. Experience suggests that an initial investment in properly focused training produces greater results.

Curriculum

Courses which drew on the statements for mathematics in the Desirable Outcomes for Learning, the relevant sections of the programmes of study of the National Curriculum for Mathematics and existing schemes of work in the early years produced effective curriculum outline maps. Work began to take account of the Reception content of the Framework for Mathematics of the National Numeracy Strategy. This was in development at the start of the pilots. Future work will need to dovetail to the objectives described in the Reception framework.

Curricula in the most effective programmes were not re-written from scratch but selected a clearly focused and manageable set of learning objectives from these frameworks. There was no attempt to cover the entire early years mathematics curriculum. The curriculum outlines were drawn up with the maths inspector or adviser and provided a common framework for all courses locally. The curriculum 'mapped' the teaching that was to occur across the three strands in:

- *the children's sessions;*

- *the joint sessions;*

- *the adults' sessions: parental support for numeracy development; adults' own numeracy improvement programme.*

In the most effective programmes objectives for the children's sessions were selected which:

- *developed both specified areas of mathematical content and the ability to solve problems through choosing and using appropriate maths;*

- *included a focus on the systematic development of mathematical language;*

- *did not give undue emphasis to any one aspect of early years numeracy e.g. sorting;*

- *extended informal competences and introduced conventions only when appropriate e.g. standard ways of representing numbers.*

Where the children's sessions focused on the completion of number sentences and other closed tasks their motivation was less. The links between the children's and joint sessions were more difficult to make.

For the adults the objectives included:

- *an understanding of early numeracy development;*

- *an understanding of how to spot new learning and recognise what to move children on to;*

- *the role of language in the acquisition of maths concepts;*

- *the role of games and play and everyday routines in developing numeracy;*

- *development of their own numeracy within number and calculation and other areas of maths, as appropriate.*

Where the objectives for the adult sessions were not explicitly outlined in the curriculum maps and/or lesson plans the sessions lacked focus. These tended to operate as support 'clinics' responding to individual difficulties within the group as they arose. Progress appeared slower and there was little evidence of direction to the learning.

In the most effective curriculum planning at least part of the work for each session followed a consistent theme across all three strands.

The curriculum was firmly structured and rigorously implemented. Where courses deviated from the main objectives to follow individual interests, direction and momentum was lost.

Sample 'Modular' Curriculum Map – Northamptonshire LEA

	Children	Adults	Together
Maths in the home	Ordering and comparing – qualitative – **Measuring: time & weighing** Language – bigger, later etc	Language Best Value Budgeting **Cooking** Packaging Telling the time/date	Planning meal/party Language Looking in cupboards **Weights in surprising containers Cooking together** Activities that can be done at home, in the car: spot the shape; the number; time.
Games and play	**Pattern:** grids; tiling; numbers; 'regularity'; matching shapes; dominoes; cards; dice.	Number patterns Symmetry Making and Developing Games Playing Games (Multicultural Games)	Noticing pattern Developing patterns Playing games Snap, Snakes & Ladders and other games
Money	What is it worth? **Use of real money** Making certain amounts up to 10p Comics Pocket money	**Budgeting** Lottery Savings Cost of living Percentages	Bring £1 worth of change – using 'real money' **Shopping trips** Money familiarity Auctioning sweets Spending with your child Budgeting with a child – jobs for money
Maths in the environment	**Comparisons use non-standard measures including capacity – qualitative** Routes/features on simple maps Shapes 2D/ 3D – language Classification Regular covering Numbers	Standard units and their use Ratio Use of scale/maps Use of timetables Language of shape	Using scales, tapes, to quantify comparisons Cooking – adapting recipes Maps and timetables Planning a trip – e.g. an outing Making plans/diagrams Maps to convey information Shapes for packaging Tessellation/tiling Playing with numbers 'the sum of the car number plate'

Teaching approaches and contexts

The Programmes that worked best used teaching approaches that had some elements common across the three strands. The most effective approaches included **setting explicit targets for learning at the beginning of each session** and consolidating and confirming learning at the end of sessions. They included whole group, small group, pair and individual work appropriate to the tasks and need. They offered **a clear structure to each session** which was explained and consistent throughout the course. In this way parents and children knew what to expect and what the purpose of what they were doing was.

The approaches adopted, employed **a range of questioning techniques** which stimulated mental calculation and fluency, maths talk and progress in applying concepts. They provided a balance of hands on and mental activity.

The **Sefton LEA** pilot concentrated on the role that modelling of dialogue and behaviour can play in the early numeracy development of young children. The kind of interactions, therefore, which are more likely to lead to progress in numeracy were the focus of the joint sessions.

Week 1
The role of the adult in providing a model to their children:

- Board games
- Playground games.

From Week 2
The parents observed the teachers:

- preparing the children for their activities;
- making seemingly unattractive activities attractive;
- listening to and accepting suggestions from the children;
- celebrating their achievements.

Parents and children then worked together.

All sessions included:

- a shared book
- number rhymes
- usually role play

▶ ***The separate sessions for adults included:***

Week 1 Introduction

- *How young children learn maths?*
- *The role of adults in providing maths opportunities and in supporting learning.*
- *The maths curriculum in school and how it is planned?*

Week 2 Promoting Maths through Dialogic Play

Week 3 Promoting Maths through Role Play

Week 4 Developing Maths through Text and Rhyme

Week 5 Number

Week 6 Shape

Weeks 7, Measuring 8, and 9

Week 10 Pattern.

Some of the courses used a range of contexts while others chose a single context. The South Tyneside project focused all the joint sessions on making and using board and card games at home. The pilot with the two and three year olds in Sefton put a strong emphasis on developing numeracy through imaginative play often stimulated by reading fiction. The Dudley pilot used construction as the stimulus for purposeful maths learning.

Apart from the value in capturing the interest and motivation of the families taking part, the choice of context does not seem to be crucial to progress. Not all the programmes that chose a single unifying context were among those that achieved greater progress. Similarly there was no correlation between the programmes offering a range of contexts for learning and progress.

The range of contexts for the children's and joint sessions included the use of:

- computer maths games and simulation software;
- board and card games;
- toys and construction kits;
- roleplay areas;
- story and books;
- sand and water 'play';
- cooking;
- the street and the environment;
- shopping – real and role;
- visits to supermarkets and other workplaces to see how maths is used;
- lunch/snack breaks as maths opportunities;
- use of early school mathematics equipment to solve tasks and problems;
- use of number lines, squares and arrays to solve tasks and problems.

The range of contexts for the adult sessions included the use of:

- 'realia' and real contexts, such as sorting out loan arrangements and calculating repayments, shopping, planning holidays etc.;
- maths for work;
- card and other games;
- data handling: graphical and statistical information in text;
- ICT such as Excel, graphs and spreadsheets, and maths practice software;
- weekly group lunch budgeting and preparation;
- making maths games equipment, and other activities for the children;
- discussion of observations in joint sessions or at home, discussion of the role of play, talk, hands on experience etc. in mathematical development;
- the use of fly on the wall video clips of classroom practice to observe learning.

Norfolk LEA Curriculum

Adults	Joint	Children
Mental maths	Designing T – shirts	Mental maths
Early counting skills	Going on a number hunt	Measuring and comparing
Strategies for problem solving	Using numbers in the environment	Number rhymes
Maths in the environment	Easter egg hunt	Estimating
Developing maths play activities	Number songs	Carrying out surveys
Measuring	Trip to the theatre to see Humpty Dumpty	Problem solving
Using a maths gadget box	At the cafe – preparation of and role play	Smarties maths
An introduction to Numberpower	Making homes to fit a special toy	Playing games
Using metric and imperial measures	Parachute games (colours, shape, counting)	Making story maps using positional/directional language
Home activities – opportunities for maths at home	The Teddy Bears Party	Role play e.g. Bakers Shop/ Health Centre
	At the seaside (role play)	Model making, as part of number track game
	Puppet making	
	Family maths book	

Other Family Numeracy programmes offered a single vocational context. In Dudley the adults were involved with Dudley College's Curriculum Construction Centre in designing and making pieces of equipment for maths areas of the children's classrooms. The development of the adults' numeracy arose from the construction work where they were taught the underpinning skills they needed to cost, calculate materials needed and measure with accuracy. Related areas of measurement were taught and the adults achieved the unit of measurement in Numberpower at either Entry Level or Level 1. Involvement and understanding in how to promote their children's numeracy came through deciding which equipment would be most appropriate and why, and then using what was made.

Sample Curriculum Map of Adult Sessions – Dudley LEA and College

Week	Home support – learning early maths concepts	Construction activities/numeracy
1	Induction/Enrolment Video of children in Nursery Introduction by Early Years Teacher to basic maths concepts Discuss a maths lending library using the small learning games made in the course Home Activities Questionnaire	*Understanding of metric and imperial measurement* *Measure everyday items for practice in accuracy and recording* Measure and cut strips of wood to size Introduce activities in construction Make bench hook Discuss accreditation
2	Introduce Look and Match game Suggestions for how to use the game – various activities Shapes, sorting, matching	Make a pan stand Discuss the main project – sequence of work Suggestions for small learning games *Select one and start preparing quantities and materials* *Exercises on area*
3	Early mass and other measuring activities	Commence the construction of learning games – dominoes, boats, cubes Discuss colour, types of paint etc. *Introduce weight and volume*
4	Early pattern/sequencing activities	Continue games – design storage boxes Prepare sketches of main project *Discuss and research cost of materials for main project* *Calculate and cost materials*
5	Time activities	Continue storage boxes for games Plan scheme of work for main project Discuss individual ideas for a learning game *Weight and learning games*
6	Early counting through rhymes	Start construction of main project Complete the learning games

7	Numeracy through books and activities coming from stories	Complete main project and paint Completion of games
8	Early number recognition activities	Information Technology Evaluation Home Activities Questionnaire Site main project in school

Adult Sessions

The provision for adults on the Family Numeracy courses has two aims. The aim of being able to help their children more fully with their numeracy development has proven to act as an incentive for adults to step back into improving their own numeracy. The pilot programmes have demonstrated that these two aims can be fulfilled. They complement and support each other.

The most effective provision for adults was seen when numeracy sessions were introduced right from the beginning and not bolted on later in the course. Projects reported difficulty where they tried to ensure continuation onto an accredited Numberpower course after the other two strands had been developed. When Numberpower students are recruited from the original Family Numeracy group, only those who have a certain level of confidence and skill appear to put themselves forward. No Entry Level students were evident in the follow on groups.

Experience from the pilot shows that trained basic skills tutors should be involved in the initial process of setting up the course. They can begin to build a relationship with the parents in the school or nursery and this increases recruitment and retention.

Adult sessions worked best where there was a clear curriculum outline or scheme of work for the whole group. The curriculum was shared with the parents so that the direction of the course was evident to them.

A sample curriculum outline from Sefton LEA	
Week 1	Student Assessment
Weeks 2 and 3	Place Value and Four Rules of Number
Week 4	Everyday Fractions
Week 5	Decimal Place Value
Week 6	Percentages
Weeks 7 and 8	Information presented in Tables/Graphs
Weeks 9 and 10	Measurement

The curriculum or scheme of work was differentiated through Individual Action or Learning Plans based on initial individual assessment. There was ongoing review of progress.

Where the value of offering valid accreditation to adults is recognised, achievement is greater. For many adults this will be a first certificate; national accreditation in numeracy should be offered. However the process of collecting evidence for accreditation should not act as a replacement for teaching the underpinning numeracy skills the group needs. Where this was the case, the rate of retention and accreditation was lower. In the most rigorous courses the completion of assignments and collation of information for portfolio based accreditation was encouraged at home. This left more time for skills teaching in the sessions.

In the most successful adult sessions, pair, small and whole group work was used as well as individual work. This encouraged among other skills the use of mathematical language when problem solving. In programmes where participants are using English as an Additional Language this takes on even greater significance if the adults are to support the early development of mathematical language in English in their children. There were opportunities for adults to share their own mental strategies with the group and evaluate them. There were opportunities to practice underpinning skills and strategies and apply them to authentic tasks.

The preparation for joint sessions occurred prior to each session and was practical in nature. The lesson is, don't just discuss it, do it! In one session, observed as part of the evaluation, the parents read a story (in pairs) from a picture book that had a number focus. They discussed the opportunities for drawing out the numeracy and mathematical aspects. They were tasked to formulate questions, devise simple roleplay scenarios, sequencing and

problem solving tasks based on the story and identify the concepts and mathematical vocabulary that would be promoted by the activities. They prepared any resources needed but were encouraged to try and use only things that would be around their house normally. The understanding of **how to promote numeracy development for their children was planned** and did not become a more casual reflection on the joint sessions.

Weekly feedback from the home activities helped to develop recognition of the learning that was going on at home. It encouraged a gathering pace to establishing home routines. Similarly feedback from the early years teacher to the adult group helped parents to recognise patterns of development in maths and not just attribute their children's statements to idiosyncrasy. Each week the Early Years teacher gave the parents examples of the kinds of things their children had said and done in the numeracy tasks. An explanation of what these meant in developmental terms was given and the parents discussed ways of moving the children on at home.

On the most effective courses guidance to further courses, accreditation or training was available early on and throughout the course.

Sample Adult Session – Northamptonshire LEA

Session 11 (9.30am – 12.30pm)

Metric and Imperial Measures/Using The Robins Café

AIMS

- To revise and consolidate work covered so far on units of measure
- To consider approximate conversions between the metric and imperial systems for everyday purposes
- To undertake practical measuring activities

OUTCOMES

By the end of the session, group members should:

- have revised the structure of the metric system (based on multiples of 10);
- have discussed when conversion between the systems of measure is required;
- have practised converting metric to imperial and vice versa;
- have carried out practical length measuring and weighing in both systems (in preparation for accreditation);
- have completed written activities if appropriate.

PLAN

9.30 - 9.35   Welcome and aims of the session

9.35 - 9.40   Accreditation update

- Collect in 'Uniform' 305.2/305.3
- All assignments for Unit 305 have now been set etc.

9.40 - 10.00   Organisation of café use for joint session

- Discuss café roles
- Parents to write role-play cards – *Brainstorm*
- Key Language for the cafe – *Flipchart*
- Keep by cafe on flipchart as a reminder
    - how much?   – change
    - more than   – which coins?
    - less than   – enough

10.00 - 10.30 Metric/Imperial Conversions

- When might approximate conversions be necessary?
- Draw out   – Material lengths
            – Weights of parcels
- Refer back to approximate conversion handout
- Question sheet

10.30 – 11.00 Practical/Written Activities

- Paired or Individual work
  - Salt dough   - Café curtains

Skill Sheets (Numberwork Direct Level 1) p50 - 55 then p71, 72

Written sheets - Truffles 306.3 / Shelving 306.2

Joint Session
11.00 – 11.45   Using the Robins Café

- Parents to start by guiding the idea of role-play / dressing up
- Start using the café together at appropriate point

11.45 – 12.00   Evaluation

Materials:
card for role plays, calculators, flour, salt, jugs, scales, dressing-up clothes, bowls, steel rule, tape measure

Basic Skills in Maths – Llewellyn and Greer

Summary of group work for display

'learnt to use metric at home and managed to adapt simple things like recipes and measuring'

'The course helped me in many ways, showing me how to help my son with maths to make it fun and interesting in ways he could understand '

'Since starting the course I have found that we have been counting and sorting and measuring things every day which is very useful for both of my children'

'. . . how easy it is to incorporate maths into daily activities'

'. . . didn't realise already doing maths every day'

Children's Sessions

Effective sessions for the children were characterised by the following features:

- a clear structure that was maintained in each session using a format that included:
  - whole group introduction which set out the target learning for the session;
  - an introductory session that modelled the skills and concepts to be worked on;
  - clear links between the children's activities and the work they were doing with their parents and at school;
  - small group, paired and individual tasks as appropriate to the skills and concepts being worked on and opportunities for children to articulate their thinking;
  - a final session that focused the learning through a final game, rhyme, song etc. and checked understanding;

- preparing children for the joint sessions or following up from these by working on the same target numeracy objectives in other contexts;

- a focus on both knowing and applying concepts and skills;

- a focus on acquiring mathematical language and number concepts through practical activities;

- a focus on using questioning techniques to:
  - extend dialogue about the maths involved in an activity;
  - begin to develop mental fluency;

- where provision included children using English as an Additional Language a stronger explicit focus was needed on:
  - understanding and using the target mathematical language;
  - focusing on its precise meaning in mathematics compared to its everyday usage, as appropriate;
  - extending opportunities for repetition in context of that language, for example, through songs, chants, games, rhymes.

The sample sessions from the Sheffield LEA Family Numeracy pilot are taken from the series that made up their scheme of work for the programme. Each session had objectives drawn from the Reception and Year 1 curriculum. Each demonstrates a restricted range of objectives giving it a clear and manageable focus for the children and the parents. The learning objectives were delivered in two children's sessions and two joint sessions on the same day. The joint sessions mirror the work the children have done separately. They lead into simple activities for home that will consolidate the learning in the course sessions.

Sheffield LEA Family Numeracy Child Session

Number Squares 1

What's My Number? (Introduction)

Use the 100 board and the 1-20 discs.
Secretly choose a number.
The children ask questions to find out which one it is.
Only YES or NO answers are allowed.
After each question eliminate numbers by taking them off the board.
What are good questions to ask?
Children could take turns to choose a number.

Missing Numbers

Use 1-20 or 1-28 number grids and numbers and fill in the missing numbers.
What number comes after/before _____ ?

Teddy Grids

Children share a 6 x 6 grid and a set of number cards 1 – 36.
Each child has a set of the same coloured teddies.
Turn over a number and put a teddy on that number.
Try and get 4 teddies in a row.

Hide A Number

Sit round a 1-100 number carpet.
Cover a number, what could it be?
How do you know?
What is the number before/after?

Conclusion

Play a group game of Hide a number.

Number Squares 2

Count In 5s (Introduction)

As a group count in 5s together using a large 100 number board.
Now count in 10s. What do you notice?

Teddy Bingo

Play a game of bingo.
Play on a grid of random numbers.
When one of your numbers is called out, cover it with a teddy.
Try and cover all your numbers.
First child to cover all their numbers calls out TEDDY!

5s And 10s

On a 100 square, count in 5s and 10s and colour in.
What pattern do you notice?
What do you notice about the numbers?

Play The Teddy Game

In pairs throw a dice and play the Teddy game.

Rhymes And Songs

A square dance
My hat it has three corners

Resources
- Teddy game
- 1 – 20, 1 – 28, 1-100 grids
- 100 square (carpet)
- Number tiles
- Teddies
- Monty computer program
- Coloured pencils

Sheffield LEA Family Numeracy Joint Session

Number Squares 1

The aim of the session is to help children to recognise numbers to 30. We want children to count, recognise and write numbers confidently to 30 and to know which number comes next.

Children find the numbers from 10-20 particularly difficult and need lots of practice in counting and writing.

Introduction – Bingo

In child/parent pairs play a game of bingo together.
Explain the method of playing.
Encourage children to recognise the numbers.

Make A Bingo Game

In child/parent pairs make a bingo card.
Decide which numbers to use and which position to put them in. Children write the numbers. Join with another pair and play a game.

4 In A Row

Make a 4 in a row game.
Numbers should be placed randomly on the grid.
Make two sets of matching number cards.
Play a game by taking it in turns to turn over a number card and place a counter over a corresponding number on the grid.
Try to get 4 in a row.
Play another game by choosing 2 number cards and either add or subtract the numbers.
Place a counter over the answer.

Conclusion – take them off!

Take the numbers off a 1-100 board and distribute them between child/parent pairs.
(Just use the numbers 1-30).
Children replace them in order.

Number Squares 2

Introduction – Sit Down!

Each child and each parent should be given a number between 1-30
All stand up.
Sit down when your number is called out.

Missing Numbers

Use a 1-20 or 1-30 number grid with some numbers missing.
Use number cards to complete the grid.
Talk about 'what number comes next?'

Ladders And Snakes!

Play a game of snakes and ladders but this time start at 100 and count back.
Go up the snakes and down the ladders!

Conclusion

Play another game of 'Sit Down.'
Use the carpet tiles and concentrate on 'teen numbers.'

Things To Do At Home

Play bingo games
Fill in missing number
Say a number and ask 'what comes next?'
Practise counting to 30

Rhymes And Songs

A square dance
My hat it has three corners

Questions To Ask

'Which number comes next?'
'Which number is missing?'
'How do you know?'
'Which number comes before or after?'

Try and use these words

Before, after, next, one more, one less, digit.

Joint sessions

Effective joint session were characterised by the use of:

- 'models' for the parents in developing strategies for:
  - using opportunities for numeracy development that are enjoyable;
  - using activities that need dialogue in order to complete them;
  - identifying misconceptions and providing further experiences which promote further thinking instead of always 'giving' the right answer;
  - giving thinking time and prompting a response;
  - praising specifically based on the mathematical objective of the task and so telling the child what they can now do or know;
  - identifying learning and knowing how to build on that as a parent in the home context;
  - using activities which do not just require children to recall facts;
  - using activities which do require children to recall facts but in an enjoyable context e.g. games, rhymes, chants;

- 'authentic' real world activities which were familiar to both parents and children;

- both home and school contexts;

- problem solving activities which allowed for more than a single 'correct' solution;

- activities which gave the children a chance to explain their thinking and talk about the maths they were doing to their parents;

- a range of organisational groupings which included whole group, small group, paired parent and child activity;

- activities which made clear the purposefulness of skills being learned;

- activities that provided a lead into home activity e.g. through the use of games and maths activity at snack times, sharing even and uneven numbers of biscuits or an apple, pouring the juice and so on.

Devon LEA – Sample Joint Sessions

First Session – Counting

Stimulus – Story of Three Billy Goats Gruff

Objectives
- To be able to count up to 3
- To be able to arrange a set of objects in order of size
- To know the language of first, second and third and be able to use it

9.00-10.00 Parents and children workshop

Everyone together for a dramatised reading of the story. Then children will be involved in the re-telling of it and questions will follow on the ordinal and cardinal aspects of the numbers to 3 e.g.

Which was the first goat? second?

Which goat went last?

How many goats have crossed the bridge so far?

(approx. 15-20 minutes)

Parents will then choose from a number of activities, including making some resources to use at home.
1. A set of large hooves with the numerals 1, 2, 3 on them and a set with corresponding dots to practise stepping on and matching with counting
2. A 3 Billy Goats Gruff and Troll board game with a 1, 2, 3 dots dice
3. Re-tell the story with a set of toy goats, plastic bridge etc.
4. Number puzzles and lotto type games
5. Counting book
   (approx 40 minutes)

10.00-10.15 Break

Children will be involved in pouring drink into large, medium, small cups and sharing out pieces of fruit and counting onto plates (one child to start a tally chart).

10.15-11.45 Parents to TV room for feedback on the session

e.g. What were the children learning? What does counting involve? Discussion led by Helen
(approx 15-20 minutes)

Jenny and Lesley then discuss aspects of the Basic Skills Agency Family Numeracy Questionnaire with the parents and assess their attitude towards mathematics and where they think their children develop numerical skills - at school/at home/both etc.

Children remain in library for own teacher-led activities.

Story Time *'Hairy McClary'*

Focus on counting 1, 2, 3

Discussion on triangular cloth – shape, edges, size when folded, etc. prior to story

Re-tell story with three sets of bowls, dogs and dog biscuits

Children to match and sort

Count out certain numbers of biscuits

Language focus on number names, same, more, less, large, medium, small

How many (1 more and 1 less - more able)

10.45   Various activities to reinforce the concepts

Washing line of numeral cards 1, 2, 3 - matching cardinal and ordinal aspects of objects

1. Role play informal with the items used in the story

2. Painting 1/2/3/4 spots on cutouts of dalmatians and matching

3. Activity sheet matching different sized dogs to bowls and biscuits

4. Number jigsaws and puzzle games

11.45-12.00 Parents join back for interactive songs and rhymes focusing on counting

e.g. 5 speckled frogs

'Ideas for Parents' Activity Sheet to enable parents to help their children with learning to count at home

Session 9
Objectives

- To solve simple real life problems involving addition and subtraction

- To begin to solve simple practical real life problems involving division (sharing) and multiplication

- To count and order numbers to at least 10

- To be able to use mathematics as an integral part of the activities demonstrating understanding through the use of appropriate language and actions

Literacy Links – *'The Doorbell Rang'* – Pat Hutchins

9.00-10.00 – Parents and Children – story session

Tell the story with everyone sitting in a circle. Retell it using the children as the characters, around a central cloth. Give each child a numeral so they are numbered and as the story unfolds they have to come out in order. Each time using real biscuits ask how many they will have each and share them out. Also question children on how many children are sitting around the table, how many are still sitting in the circle, etc? Will each child get more or less biscuits as others arrive? Are there more or less children sitting around the table? etc.

Parent and children activities

Activities will focus on real life problem-solving situations involving the operations.

Six tables will be set up, with "scenarios" on cards for parents to read out to their children and work with them to solve, using the objects and equipment provided. Activities will revise themes previously covered and have extensions.

Problem

1. Four teddy bears buy a packet of sweets. Can the sweets be shared equally so they get the same number each? How many sweets does each get? Are any left?

   What if another teddy came along? What if they had — more sweets?

   Can you sort them?

2. — cars are waiting to fill up with petrol at the garage. Can they line up at the pumps so there is the same number at each pump? How many altogether?

   How many are at each pump?

   What if 6 more arrive? Which car is in front/behind, first, second, etc?

3. The farmer wanted to share his animals equally among his fields so they each get enough grass to eat. Can you sort the animals equally among the fields?

   If the sheep and horses can't go together how could you sort them now?

   How many are in each field?

   How many altogether?

4. The teddies were making some buns. They needed to share the cake mixture equally into — buns to fill the tray. Can you help them to share it equally so there is enough for each bun?

   How many buns can you make?

   If there are 4 teddies, how many buns will they get each?

   If two more teddies join them, how many buns could they then have each?

5. There are – train carriages. There are 3 engines. Can you share the carriages out equally between the engines? How many carriages will each train have? How many are there altogether? Which one is in front/behind?

6. Can you make a tall tower using all of these cubes. Can you break it in half, into 2 equal smaller towers?

   How many cubes are in each one? etc.

   Can you make 3 towers of different lengths? How are they different? Which one is the longest/shortest?

10.15   Parents leave for own session
Focus on *average, mean, mode, median.*
(Multiplication and division problems)

Children's session and break
Read the 'Hungry Caterpillar' – retell sharing out the fruit mentioned in the story with the children. Ask whether there are enough pieces of fruit for each child. Focus on language of more/less, equal, the same, share, divide, groups.

10.30   Activities

1. Sequence parts of the story, matching the fruit with the numerals.

2. Sort a range of different sized caterpillars into large, small, medium. How many of the large caterpillars can fit on the large leaf?

   What about the small leaf?
   How many more can fit on to the large leaf than the small leaf?

3. Free play with:
   - sorting sets
   - jigsaws, sequencing puzzles
   - caterpillars and leaves

4. Matching sets of the same number with numerals and pictorial representations, e.g. pictures of fruit.

5. Solving simple number problems (more able – solving addition and subtraction sums involving the symbols for the operations, e.g. caterpillars on leaves).

11.45-12.00 Back together for counting songs

'I always thought of maths as just adding and subtracting that you had to try and learn to do on paper. It always felt like just doing sums and hoping to keep up. I never knew quite what to do and just got out of it as soon as I could. When my eldest started coming to me with his homework I really started to think how can I help him? I don't understand this myself.'

'This course has taught us that starting maths isn't just about adding and sums it's about sorting and matching and sequencing and counting and measuring. You don't learn these things by just sitting at a table with pages of numbers. We have played games, read stories, done role-playing, sung songs, played clapping games.'

'I'm far more into it all. I've made a lot of progress with my own maths and suddenly some of the pennies have dropped. Decimals I never knew what the point was for. I never realised that it's the same as money. I am keen to go on with it and try and get the certificate.'

'When Mark comes to me now I am able to sit down and have a go at helping him with his maths. Even with him I try to think of ways we can practise the maths he's doing in a real way. The other day he brought some work about adding centimetres and working out how many metres and centimetres. I thought he doesn't see the point of this. We have always needed a shelf in the kitchen which I never made. I thought let's have a go. So we worked out how much we needed and how much it was going to cost. We went out got some chipboard, measured it all up and cut it right and we did the shelf together.'

Encouraging home routines

The overall picture in the pilots was of a statistically significant increase on all items in the home activities questionnaire. There was one exception to this where there was little room for increase in the activity. Within this general picture there were differences in the extent to which the pilots achieved increases in the frequency and the range of numeracy-related home routines.

The greatest number of pilot programmes showed significant progress in activities relating to sorting things in the house into groups, capacity related activity at bath-time, singing number songs, playing card and board games, recognising numbers in the environment including prices and reading number and counting books. Some pilots achieved significant increases on a wider range of activities.

To identify what kind of practice leads to the most progress for the parents in their support for their children we have examined:

(a) the kind of activity in which the greatest increases were stimulated overall;

(b) the kind of activity in which the greatest increases were stimulated in the greatest number of pilot programmes;

(c) the nature of the joint sessions;

(d) the nature of the 'bridging' activities between sessions.

The tendency is for the greatest increases to occur where there were well managed joint sessions which demonstrated the characteristics outlined in the section *Successful strategies – case studies and lessons – Joint sessions.*

Beyond this we can identify a number of other features which, when incorporated into the programme, contribute to successfully changing the level of numeracy related activity at home. In addition it is clear that the use of certain home-loan practices do not stimulate the same level of activity as others. Printed handouts, with lists of ideas and explanations of what to do and why, do not engender the kinds of changes that other more focused practices do. They have a purpose when carefully constructed and checked for readability in supporting other practices but do not stand alone as an effective means of supporting parents to help their children.

Effective 'bridging' activities included:

- **take home early numeracy 'toolkits'.** These took a variety of forms including PACT style wallets and plastic toolboxes. Typically each family was given a range of everyday items for parents and children to use at home as numeracy resources. During the course parents were encouraged to add to the 'kit' and customise it to meet the needs and interests of their children. The 'starter kits' contained items including:
  - a selection of buttons, assorted sizes;
  - shoe laces/ribbon/tape – different lengths and widths;
  - a collection of beads/marbles;
  - numerals cut from catalogues, etc.;
  - a small pack of plain cards to develop into a game;
  - a piece of card with boxes on one side to be used to make a board game;
  - pieces of card of different sizes/shapes, eg, labels, tickets, squares, rectangles, triangles;
  - counters;
  - dice;

- **home loan games changed weekly** including some games made in workshops, games prepared by teaching staff and commercial games. Some of the pilots obtained some small sponsorship funds to develop a bank of games;

- **IMPACT sheets and materials**[13];

- supporting number rhyme booklets and tapes;

- supporting vocabulary booklets.

The presence of additional accreditation through OCN Parents as (Numeracy) Educators was a feature of some of the programmes with the highest overall progress against all the three aims.

---

13. *Sharing Maths Cultures*, IMPACT, Merttens and Vass, The Falmer Press, 1990; IMPACT University of North London, Scholastic, 1994

Cost effectiveness

Each programme received £10,000 to develop and implement the pilot course in their authority. This was match funded to a minimum of a further £5,000 by the partnership. The local partnership secured further funding from a variety of sources including the LEA, Further Education Funding Council, Training and Enterprise Council and Education Business Partnerships.

With the finance provided the programmes were effective in boosting the children's numeracy and the parents' ability to help their children. This effect was quantifiable. Both parents and children had benefited and the expenditure on the provision can be considered as giving double value.

The pilot programmes were deliberately experimental, varying in many aspects. This included the number of hours offered and the ratio of separate to joint sessions. The range of costs per course given below incorporates all the development costs of an entirely new initiative. The anticipated costs or further courses is less since many of the materials, planning, promotional and other setting up costs will not be incurred to the same extent.

The costs per course ranged between £1,000 featuring a low ratio of separate sessions over fewer hours and £7,500 for the most costly and longest courses.

Continuation – broadening the impact of family numeracy

The Family Numeracy courses had an immediate impact on the families that had taken part. Many of the participating LEAs devised strategies for widening the impact in the schools where the pilots were based and also across the authority. The aim was to disseminate and embed **elements** of the successful practices that had been devised and tested within the pilots. The approaches and materials that were developed were 'mined' for their potential to inform and involve parents who do not have numeracy needs themselves but want to be able to further support their children.

Within the schools that ran Family Numeracy courses there is a legacy of parental involvement. There is a commitment to parental partnership and offering opportunities to parents to improve their skills. The schools plan to use the materials and approaches developed in the courses to work with other groups of parents in workshops and parents meetings. A number of the schools have created permanent numeracy-game and activity 'bags' as a home loan resource to be used in much the same way as PACT systems. Others have a repertoire of numeracy activities developed around story books which can be incorporated into book bags to go home. Some are extending the materials which were produced for promoting mental fluency and the recall of number facts through home activities so that they can be introduced to the parents of other year groups. The ideas for these materials are being shared across the authority and will form part of the measures for involving parents within the implementation of the National Numeracy Strategy.

NFER Report on the Family Numeracy Evaluation

by Dr Greg Brooks and Dougal Hutchison

Main Finding

Participants made statistically significantly more progress than controls on both parts of the Baseline Assessment and overall (effect size = 0.36).

Summary

Data were received for just over 500 families on 53 courses.

Baseline Assessment data were received for the following numbers of children:

	beginning of course	end of course	with data on both occasions
participants – all	274	241	215
– in same areas as controls	161	155	148
controls	165	156	144

Table 1: Numbers of participating and control children in control-group areas for whom Baseline data were received for both beginning and end of course and, for each group, the average scores and standard deviations for each half of and the full test, for both occasions

	Participants (N = 148)		Controls (N = 144)	
	beginning	end	beginning	end
Number (max. = 4)				
average score	2.09	2.91	1.92	2.35
(s.d.)	(1.10)	(1.20)	(1.14)	(1.15)
Mathematical language (max. = 4)				
average score	1.79	2.68	1.71	2.19
(s.d.)	(1.08)	(1.08)	(1.22)	(1.21)
Total (max. = 8)				
average score	3.89	5.59	3.63	4.55
(s.d.)	(1.93)	(2.12)	(2.17)	(2.16)

Report

1. Amount of information

Data were received from 53 courses.

Course Data Forms were received from 51 courses, Tutor Questionnaires from 38 courses, Teacher Questionnaires from 41 courses, and aggregated Home Activities Questionnaires for the beginning and end of 52 courses.

For the numbers recruited onto the courses, the Course Data Forms gave a total of 517 parents and 515 children. However, some of the more detailed data were missing because not all courses sent in Profiles, so that the numbers of these received were 411 for parents and 418 for participating children. On the latter basis, it seems that seven parents for whom Profiles were received had more than one participating child.

The numbers of children for whom Baseline Assessment data were received are shown in Table 2.

	beginning of course	end of course	with data on both occasions
participants – all	274	241	215
– in same areas as controls	161	155	148
controls	165	156	144

The number of participating children for whom Baseline data were received was significantly smaller than the total participating. This was because many children were too young to be assessed on the Baseline instrument.

General characteristics are reported in section 8 below for the 411 parents and 418 participating children for whom Profiles were received; but Baseline data were analysed only for children for whom such data were available for both the beginning and the end of the course – and those numbers were in turn smaller than those for whom data were available for each occasion separately, because of missing data.

2. Baseline assessment – all relevant participants – descriptive statistics and significance of differences

Baseline data were available for both beginning and end of the course for 215 participating children. Table 3 gives the distribution of scores for each of the eight items in the Numeracy Baseline instrument for those children, and for beginning and end of the course separately. The Table shows the numbers and percentages of children who were assessed as having achieved each item.

Table 3: Numbers and percentages of participating children assessed as achieving items on Baseline Assessment, beginning and end of course (Total N = 215)

	beginning		end	
	N	(%)	N	(%)
Number				
Sorts objects	194	(90)	202	(94)
Counts objects	130	(61)	178	(83)
Aware of addition	87	(41)	150	(70)
Solves problems	30	(14)	79	(37)
Mathematical language				
Describes size	169	(79)	202	(94)
Describes position	129	(60)	181	(84)
Numbers to 10	47	(22)	114	(53)
Explains addition	28	(13)	62	(29)

Table 4 gives the distribution, average and standard deviation of participating children's scores for each half of and the full Baseline instrument, for the beginning and end of the courses.

Statistical tests were carried out on the differences between the average scores for beginning and end of the course, for each half-test and the full test, and on the differences in the percentages achieving each item on the two occasions. The percentage of participating children assessed as achieving an item increased significantly on all individual items (see next section for a small difference in this respect when participants outside control-groups areas were dropped). Participating children also made significant gains on each half-test and overall.

Table 4: Distribution of Baseline Assessment scores for half-tests and the full test, participating children, beginning and end of course, with average scores and standard deviations (Total N = 215)

		beginning		end	
		N	(%)	N	(%)
Number	0	15	(7)	9	(4)
	1	64	(30)	30	(14)
	2	58	(27)	28	(13)
	3	51	(24)	69	(32)
	4	27	(13)	79	(37)
	average	2.05		2.83	
	(s.d.)	(1.15)		(1.19)	
Mathematical language	0	40	(19)	10	(5)
	1	44	(21)	23	(11)
	2	85	(40)	69	(32)
	3	25	(12)	54	(25)
	4	21	(10)	59	(27)
	average	1.73		2.60	
	(s.d.)	(1.18)		(1.14)	
Overall	0	7	(3)	3	(1)
	1	29	(14)	10	(5)
	2	30	(14)	14	(7)
	3	32	(15)	18	(8)
	4	37	(17)	18	(8)
	5	34	(16)	34	(16)
	6	23	(11)	37	(17)
	7	11	(5)	36	(17)
	8	12	(6)	45	(21)
	average	3.79		5.43	
	(s.d.)	(2.09)		(2.16)	

3. Baseline assessment – participants and controls in control group areas – descriptive statistics and significance of differences, overall

Not all courses had control groups; to make valid comparisons between participants and controls, participants in areas where there were no controls were dropped. In this section, only results from control children, and from participating children in the same areas, are reported. There were 148 participants and 144 controls in these areas for whom data were available for both beginning and end of the course. Table 5 gives the distribution of scores for each of the eight items in the Numeracy Baseline instrument, for participating and control children in those areas separately, and for the beginning and end of the courses separately. Like Table 3, Table 5 shows the numbers and percentages of children who were assessed as having achieved each of the separate items.

Table 5: Numbers and percentages of participating and control children in control group areas assessed as achieving items on Baseline Assessment, beginning and end of course

	Participants (Total N = 148)				Controls (Total N = 144)			
	beginning		end		beginning		end	
	N	(%)	N	(%)	N	(%)	N	(%)
Number								
Sorts objects	141	(95)	143	(97)	129	(90)	133	(92)
Counts objects	90	(61)	121	(82)	81	(56)	103	(72)
Aware of addition	59	(40)	105	(71)	50	(35)	76	(53)
Solves problems	20	(14)	62	(42)	16	(11)	27	(19)
Mathematical language								
Describes size	123	(83)	143	(97)	112	(78)	129	(90)
Describes position	97	(66)	127	(86)	81	(56)	104	(72)
Numbers to 10	31	(21)	83	(56)	38	(26)	55	(38)
Explains addition	14	(10)	43	(29)	15	(10)	28	(19)

Table 6 gives the distribution, average and standard deviation of participating and control children's scores for each half of and the full Baseline instrument, and for the beginning and end of the courses.

Table 6: Distribution of Baseline Assessment scores for half-tests and the full test, for participating and control children in control group areas, beginning and end of course, with average scores and standard deviations

| | | Participants (Total N = 148) | | | | Controls (Total N = 144) | | | |
| | | beginning | | end | | beginning | | end | |
Number		N	(%)	N	(%)	N	(%)	N	(%)
	0	6	(4)	5	(3)	12	(8)	6	(4)
	1	47	(32)	22	(15)	52	(36)	34	(24)
	2	40	(27)	16	(11)	28	(19)	33	(23)
	3	37	(25)	43	(29)	40	(28)	45	(31)
	4	18	(12)	62	(42)	12	(8)	26	(18)
average		2.09		2.91		1.92		2.35	
(s.d.)		(1.10)		(1.20)		(1.14)		(1.15)	

Mathematical language

		N	(%)	N	(%)	N	(%)	N	(%)
	0	20	(14)	4	(3)	29	(20)	14	(10)
	1	33	(22)	16	(11)	33	(23)	26	(18)
	2	65	(44)	46	(31)	46	(32)	47	(33)
	3	18	(12)	40	(27)	23	(16)	32	(22)
	4	12	(8)	42	(28)	13	(9)	25	(17)
average		1.79		2.68		1.71		2.19	
(s.d.)		(1.08)		(1.08)		(1.22)		(1.21)	

Overall

		N	(%)	N	(%)	N	(%)	N	(%)
	0	1	(1)	2	(1)	6	(4)	1	(1)
	1	18	(12)	5	(3)	27	(19)	12	(8)
	2	22	(15)	10	(7)	16	(11)	19	(13)
	3	22	(15)	11	(7)	23	(16)	14	(10)
	4	29	(20)	11	(7)	21	(15)	26	(18)
	5	25	(17)	24	(16)	17	(12)	17	(12)
	6	17	(12)	24	(16)	19	(13)	30	(21)
	7	8	(5)	27	(18)	9	(6)	6	(4)
	8	6	(4)	34	(23)	6	(4)	19	(13)
average		3.89		5.59		3.63		4.55	
(s.d.)		(1.93)		(2.12)		(2.17)		(2.16)	

Statistical tests were carried out for each half-test and the full test on the differences between participants and controls at the beginning of the course. These differences were not significant. Statistical tests were carried out, for participants and controls separately, on the differences between the average scores for beginning and end of the course, for each half-test and the full test, and on the differences in the percentages achieving each item on the two occasions. Statistical tests were also carried out on the differences in average *gain* of the two groups, for each half-test and the full test.

In terms of progress within groups, the percentage of both participating and control children assessed as achieving an item increased significantly on all individual items except Sorts Objects (which almost all children could do at the beginning anyway) – this finding differs from that for the full set of participating children.

Both participating and control children also made statistically significant gains on each half-test and overall.

> *Above all, the participating children made statistically significantly larger gains than the controls, both on Number and on Mathematical Language, and on the full Baseline instrument (effect size for full instrument = 0.36).*

4. Baseline assessment – participants and controls in control group areas – outline descriptive statistics and significance of differences, by LEA

The 148 participating children and 144 controls discussed in the previous section were drawn from 11 LEAs. This section reports data at LEA level. In one case (LEA B) the number of participants (2) was too small to permit statistical analysis. Even in the LEA with the largest numbers (LEA I, 25 participants and 21 controls), the numbers were too small to make it informative to give the distributions of scores even for the full test, still less for the half tests, or to report the numbers of children in each LEA assessed as achieving each separate item.

This section therefore gives only the average scores and standard deviations for the full test, for beginning and end of the course, for participants and controls, with the significance of the difference in *gain* (as determined by a t-test). These details are given in Table 7.

Table 7: Baseline Assessment average scores and standard deviations for half-tests and the full test, for participating and control children in control group areas, beginning and end of course, by LEA, with statistical significance of difference in gain

		Participants		Controls	
		beginning	end	beginning	end
LEA & significance					
A ns					
	N	18		9	
	average	3.39	4.89	1.89	3.22
	(s.d.)	(1.29)	(2.08)	(1.62)	(1.39)
B					
	N	2		7	
	numbers too small to permit analysis				
C *					
	N	17		19	
	average	4.12	6.29	3.79	4.79
	(s.d.)	(1.22)	(1.49)	(1.08)	(1.23)
D *					
	N	11		12	
	average	3.82	5.91	3.83	4.50
	(s.d.)	(2.09)	(2.07)	(2.12)	(1.57)
E ns (but N.B. participants' average gain was *smaller* than controls)					
	N	21		21	
	average	5.10	5.71	5.00	6.33
	(s.d.)	(1.89)	(2.10)	(2.30)	(1.77)
F *					
	N	18		19	
	average	5.72	7.89	6.05	6.53
	(s.d.)	(1.07)	(0.32)	(1.22)	(1.81)

Key: ns = non-significant

   * = statistically significant

G *					
	N	12		12	
	average	3.08	5.75	1.00	2.00
	(s.d.)	(1.38)	(1.14)	(0)	(1.28)

H ns					
	N	6		6	
	average	4.00	5.67	3.00	4.33
	(s.d.)	(2.19)	(1.75)	(1.55)	(2.07)

I *					
	N	25		21	
	average	2.12	3.40	2.14	2.76
	(s.d.)	(1.24)	(1.76)	(1.28)	(1.48)

J ns					
	N	13		12	
	average	3.62	5.31	3.33	4.08
	(s.d.)	(2.33)	(2.29)	(1.92)	(2.27)

K ns					
	N	5		6	
	average	5.00	7.20	4.17	5.50
	(s.d.)	(2.24)	(0.84)	(2.32)	(1.76)

In interpreting Table 7, it must be remembered that in all cases the numbers of children involved were small. However, within the 10 LEAs where numbers were large enough to permit some analysis, in all cases both participants' and controls' average scores increased, and in nine out of the 10 cases the difference in gain was in favour of participants. The difference was significant in five cases out of the 10, and non-significant in the other five the latter group included the one LEA where the participants made less gain than controls.

Is it possible to discern, within the 10 LEAs, any where the impact of Family Numeracy was statistically more (or less) significant than the rest? This was investigated by means of a multi-level analysis; this produced the 'LEA effects' listed in decreasing rank order in Table 8.

Table 8: LEA effects in decreasing rank order

LEA	LEA effect	2 x standard error
G*	0.74	0.66
C	0.26	0.61
F	0.22	0.60
K	0.22	0.80
D	0.15	0.68
H	-0.05	0.77
J	-0.10	0.65
A	-0.18	0.61
I	-0.50	0.56
E *	-1.01	0.58

* = statistically significantly different from rest of list

The minus signs against some of the LEA effects do not mean that the effects were negative, or even that they were below the progress of the controls (this was true in only one case, as already pointed out); the minus signs mean only that the effects were below the average of all the LEA effects. The value of twice the standard error is shown because the effect must be greater than that value (ignoring sign) to be statistically significantly different from the other effects.

Table 8 therefore shows that only LEAs G and E, at the top and bottom of the list respectively, had effects that were statistically significantly different from the rest. Tentatively, because of the small numbers, this can be interpreted as meaning that:

- in eight out of the 10 LEAs for which this analysis was possible the Family Numeracy programmes were about equally effective; and

- *the Family Numeracy programme in LEA G was the most effective, and that in LEA E the least effective*, of the 10 LEAs for which this analysis was possible.

5. Analysis of participating children's performance against background variables

Of the 215 participating children for whom there were Baseline data for both beginning and end of course, there were none for whom Profiles were not received. This section is therefore based on all 215 children. Only three background variables were available: sex, English as a first or additional language, and ethnicity. For ethnicity, because white children greatly outnumbered all others together, the dichotomy White/Other was used. The relationship calculated was between these variables and the relevant children's average gain, that is each group's average post-test score minus their average pre-test score. The numbers of children in each category are shown in Table 9, together with the average gains and the standard deviations of those gains for the full Baseline test. Information on gender was not available for 39 children.

Table 9: Participating children's attainment against background variables

	N	average gain	(standard deviation)
Boys	103	1.78	(1.28)
Girls	73	1.62	(1.49)
Children with English as			
– first language	203	1.66	(1.49)
– additional language	12	1.42	(1.08)
White children	153	1.76	(1.42)
Children of other ethnicities	62	1.37	(1.55)

None of the differences in Table 9 was statistically significant. This suggests that the initiative was equally successful for boys and girls, for monolingual and bilingual children, and for white children and those of other ethnicities.

6. General characteristics of parents and children for whom Profiles were received

Gender
Of the 411 parents, 393 were female and 13 were male (in five cases the information was not provided). Of the 418 participating children, 171 were girls and 240 were boys (in seven cases the information was not provided).

Age
The age-distributions of the parents and children are shown in Table 10. Two of the parents were in their sixties, and were presumably grandmothers.

Table 10: **Age-distributions of participating parents and children at start of course**

Parents		Children	
Age	*Number*	*Age*	*Number*
20-24	48	2	21
25-29	113	3	99
30-34	124	4	198
35-39	51	5	69
40-44	17	6	9
45 and over	15		
Not stated	43	Not stated	22
Total	411	Total	418

Ethnicity

The ethnic backgrounds of the parents and children were as shown in Table 11.

Table 11: **Ethnic backgrounds of participating parents and children**

	Parents	*Children*
White	356	350
Black		
– Caribbean	3	2
– African	6	6
– Other	0	0
Indian	16	16
Pakistani	6	6
Bangladeshi	6	6
Chinese	1	0
Other	4	10
Not stated	13	22
Total	411	418

Languages

The parents were asked to state whether they and their children spoke any language besides English and, if so, which. A total of 51 (12 per cent) of the parents and 41 (10 per cent) of the children were said to have a first language other than English, as shown in Table 12.

Table 12: Linguistic background of participants

	Parents	Children
Bengali	6	6
Gujerati	9	12
Punjabi	3	4
Urdu	8	7
Tamil	1	1
Farsi	1	1
Turkish	1	
Arabic	1	1
French	4	
Spanish	4	1
Portuguese	2	1
Italian	2	1
German	1	
Polish	1	
Serbo-Croatian	1	1
Yoruba	1	1
Tigri	3	3
Amharic	2	1
Total	51	41

Fifteen of the children were said to have had experience of writing systems other than the Roman alphabet, such as Arabic script and those used for Indian languages.

Parents' occupational status

Participating parents were asked to classify their current occupational status in one of nine categories. The categories, and the distribution of responses, were as shown in Table 13.

Table 13: Occupational status of parents

Category	Number	%
Full-time employee	12	3
Part-time employee	58	14
Full-time self-employed	3	1
Part-time self-employed	8	2
In full-time education	0	0
Unemployed	40	12
Temporarily sick/disabled	0	0
Permanently sick/disabled	4	1
Looking after home/family	222	63
Other	9	3
Total	356	100

(In 55 cases the information was not provided.)

Parents' qualifications

A total of 38 parents had fewer than 11 years' full-time education in the UK – these tended to be members of ethnic minorities. The parents' highest qualifications in mathematics and overall were classified in five categories ranging from 'below CSE/GCSE' to 'higher education', and the distribution was as shown in Table 14.

Table 14: Parents' highest qualifications in mathematics and generally

	in mathematics		generally	
	N	%	N	%
below CSE/GCSE	236	57	232	56
CSE/GCSE	120	29	60	15
O-Level	29	7	28	7
A-Level/further education	25	6	69	17
higher education	1	1	22	5
Total	411	100	411	100

For many parents, the level of qualification of those classified as having qualifications at CSE or GCSE level was barely above that of those reporting no qualifications at all; and the situation in mathematics was even more acute. Very few parents had post-16 qualifications in mathematics, though about a fifth had such qualifications generally. Only 38 parents (a different subset from that mentioned above) said they had had previous basic skills tuition.

The participating parents were therefore in general poorly qualified and not employed outside the home.

7. Course data

Aggregated course data are shown on a copy of the course data form appended to this report. Overall attendance and retention levels were high for both parents and children. Numbers of parents achieving accreditation or continuing to study are not given, because most respondents reported that this information was 'Not yet known'.

Very few parents or children were reported as having gained no benefit from the courses, and the great majority were reported to have benefited significantly or a great deal.

8. Numeracy-related home activities

Aggregated data, for both beginning and end of the course, are shown on a copy of the questionnaire appended to this report. All numeracy-related home activities showed an increase by the end of the course, and the increase was statistically significant in every case but one. The exception was 'Does your child play with construction kits/building blocks with you?' – this appeared to be very frequent before the courses.

9. Tutor and teacher questionnaires

Again, aggregated data are shown on copies of the questionnaires appended to this report. The number of responses received was 38 for the tutor questionnaire and 41 for the teacher questionnaire. In general, both tutors and teachers were positive about the factors listed, except that tutors seemed unconvinced that accreditation was important for the effectiveness of the courses.

Course Data Form

	Parents	Children
number recruited	517	515
number female	499	216
number male	18	299
number of participants for whom English was an additional language	66	55
% attendance	(average) 83%	(average) 87%
% retention	(average) 84%	(average) 87%
number achieving full or part accreditation	?	N/A
number continuing to study	?	N/A

Give numbers of the parents who have:	Not at all	A little	Significantly	A great deal
improved their numeracy skills	26	121	170	80
increased their confidence in supporting their children's numeracy	12	42	218	166
more contact with school	16	133	142	117

Based on ongoing assessment, give numbers of the children who have shown:	Not at all	A little	Significantly	A great deal
improvement in understanding of instructions and questions relating to calculating, making decisions, estimating, rounding	13	92	222	110

improvement in use of language of e.g. counting, comparison, ordering	14	74	199	144
increase in vocabulary relating to numerals, money, measures, time etc.	14	68	226	112
an increase in their confidence in dealing with numerical situations	11	60	196	155
an increase in interest in toys/games/ books/roleplay involving numbers	8	36	213	172

Numeracy-related home activities

In each box, the upper number is the number of parents giving that response at the beginning of the course, and the lower number is the number of parents giving that response at the end of the course.

It should be remembered that the overall numbers differed between the two occasions: it is differences in the *distribution* of responses that are significant.

Does your child do any of these with you?	Never	1-2 a year	1-2 a month	1 a week	2-3 a week	Every day
Sort clothes, shopping, toys etc. into groups	29 7	16 3	59 40	95 97	131 148	107 99
Count out items of shopping, toys etc.	48 14	20 2	48 3	117 102	115 141	82 96
Match items of clothing, toys, washing etc.	75 21	14 7	48 38	107 98	120 138	74 90
Sort items of shopping, toys etc. in order of size	164 41	23 10	66 67	89 129	61 108	25 36

Does your child do any of these with you?	Never	1-2 a year	1-2 a month	1 a week	2-3 a week	Every day
Sort items of shopping, toys etc. in order of **weight**	310 132	15 21	39 103	41 82	18 41	12 12
Fill and empty different size containers at bath time	44 15	6 1	29 7	60 55	172 186	125 127
Sing number songs like 10 Green Bottles	36 9	12 7	55 22	78 64	139 143	121 149
Cooking (e.g. weighing, counting out ingredients)	147 49	54 25	120 145	75 116	33 44	7 9
Play clapping games	84 26	20 10	63 63	99 92	99 118	70 94
Play games involving numbers or matching e.g. snap, bingo, board games, dominoes)	46 8	14 3	67 24	102 94	131 176	62 79
Play computer games involving numbers	203 135	23 15	36 32	50 70	59 77	56 51
Play with construction kits/building blocks	29 14	10 4	51 39	83 88	120 117	140 117

Does your child look at any of these with you?	Never	1-2 a year	1-2 a month	1 a week	2-3 a week	Every day
Numbers in the street	108 / 25	15 / 4	55 / 32	66 / 71	84 / 113	101 / 135
Shapes in the street	129 / 27	13 / 10	70 / 43	57 / 90	75 / 96	83 / 110
Calendars	192 / 73	25 / 14	62 / 71	57 / 78	39 / 52	47 / 86
Prices in shops	168 / 56	10 / 9	48 / 40	87 / 114	68 / 83	36 / 64
Number/Tell the time books	71 / 18	14 / 5	77 / 45	72 / 93	123 / 149	71 / 72

	Never	1-2 a year	1-2 a month	1 a week	More than 1 a week
How often do you go to school activities?	69 / 18	104 / 68	106 / 97	49 / 102	89 / 70
How often do you help with school activities?	171 / 78	69 / 67	68 / 58	55 / 89	58 / 70
How often do you talk with your child's teacher?	20 / 1	23 / 10	88 / 65	114 / 115	176 / 179

Tutor Questionnaire **For all items, overall N= 38.**

Please use the rating scale 1-4 with 1 representing most important and 4 least important to answer the following questions.

N.B. So few responses occurred at point 4 of the scale that responses for points 3 and 4 have been combined.

1. How important have each of the factors involved in the Family Numeracy project you have run been in creating effective provision for developing the parent's numeracy skills?

	1	*2*	*3+4*	*(No response)*
Choice of curriculum content	33	4	1	
Amount of time provision lasted (i.e. was it long enough?)	15	15	7	1
Inclusion of joint provision	28	7	2	1
Incorporating 'tasks' for home	25	12	1	
Presence of accreditation	6	8	27	4
Pre/post testing	5	14	13	6

Any others please fill in: (No item entered by more than 3 respondents)

2. How important have each of the factors involved in the Family Numeracy project you have run been in increasing the parent's ability to support their children's numeracy development?

	1	*2*	*3+4*	*(No response)*
Choice of curriculum content	34	3	1	
Amount of time provision lasted (i.e. was it long enough?)	16	17	3	2
Inclusion of joint provision	36	2	0	
Incorporating 'tasks' for home	28	9	0	1

Any others please fill in: (No item entered by more than 3 respondents)

Teacher Questionnaire   **For all items, overall N = 41.**

1. Which are the teaching approaches you have used in the Family Numeracy project which have proved effective in developing the children's numeracy skills and use and understanding of mathematical language?

Problem solving	38	Games	27
Mental maths	29	Number rhymes	33
Role-play	40	Number through story	38
Construction	31	Oral work	39

Any others please list: (No extra item listed by more than 2 respondents)

2. How important have each of the factors involved in the project you have run been in creating effective provision for developing the children's numeracy and mathematical language?

   N.B. So few responses were at point 4 of the scale that points 3 and 4 have been combined.

	1	*2*	*3+4*
Choice of curriculum content	36	3	2
Amount of time provision lasted (i.e. was it long enough?)	14	10	16
Inclusion of additional separate provision	20	17	3
Inclusion of joint provision	31	7	3
Incorporating 'tasks' for home	27	10	3
Providing parents with the opportunity to improve their own numeracy skills	17	12	11

Any others please fill in: (No extra item listed by more than 1 respondent)

3. What 'spin-offs' from involvement in the Family Numeracy project would you identify for this group of children in their approach to play and work tasks?

Improvement in confidence	40
Improvement in concentration and perseverance	36
Greater cooperation and group work skills	29
Greater eagerness to explore and initiate new learning	36
Development of simple problem solving skills	31
Improvement in general listening skills	29
Improvement in listening to instructions	31
Development in spoken vocabulary and fluency	28
Greater interest in reading	12
Greater interest in writing	10

Any others please list: (No extra item listed by more than 2 respondents)

Appendix

The Evaluation Framework

<table>
<tr><td colspan="2">Family Numeracy
Course Data Form</td><td>The
Basic Skills
Agency</td></tr>
</table>

LEA.. Course Identifier Number...

Report for period from .... to ....

Course at .... school/nursery/family centre

To be completed jointly by the early years course teacher and adult tutor

	Parents	*Children*
number recruited		
number female		
number male		
number of participants for whom English is an additional language		

	Parents	*Children*
% attendance		
% retention		
number achieving full or part accreditation		N/A
number continuing to study		N/A

Give numbers of the parents who have:	Not at all	A little	Significantly	A great deal
improved their numeracy skills				
increased their confidence in supporting their children's numeracy				
have more contact with school				

To be completed by the Early Years Family Numeracy course teacher

Based on ongoing assessment, give numbers of the children who have shown:	Not at all	A little	Significantly	A great deal
improvement in understanding of instructions and questions relating to calculating, making decisions, estimating, rounding				
improvement in use of language of e.g. counting, comparison, ordering				
increase in vocabulary relating to numerals, money, measures, time etc.				
an increase in their confidence in dealing with numerical situations				
an increase in interest in toys/games/books/roleplay involving numbers				

Family Numeracy

Home Activities Questionnaire

The
Basic Skills
Agency

Beginning/End of course   Date........................ Identifier ☐ ☐ ☐ ☐ ☐ ☐ ☐

Does your child do any of these with you?	*Never*	*1-2 a year*	*1-2 a month*	*1 a week*	*2-3 a week*	*Every day*
Sort clothes, shopping, toys etc. in order of size						
Count out items of shopping, toys etc.						
Match items of clothing, toys, washing etc.						
Sort items of shopping, toys etc. in order of size						
Sort items of shopping, toys etc. in order of weight						
Fill and empty different size containers at bath time						
Sing number songs like 10 Green Bottles						
Cooking (e.g. weighing, counting out ingredients)						
Play clapping games						
Play games involving numbers or matching e.g. snap, bingo, board games, dominoes)						

Play computer games involving numbers						
Play with construction kits/building blocks						

Does your child look at any of these with you?	Never	1-2 a year	1-2 a month	1 a week	2-3 a week	Every day
Numbers in the street						
Shapes in the street						
Calendars						
Prices in shops						
Number/Tell the time books						

	Never	1 a year	1 a month	1 a week	More than 1 a week
How often do you go to school activities?					
How often do you help with school activities?					
How often do you talk with your child's teacher?					

Family Numeracy
Assessment Course Record

Mathematics A. Number

Child identifier no.	1	2	3	4	5	6	7	8	9	10	11	12
Sorts sets of objects by given criterion and explains sorting												
Counts objects accurately												
Shows awareness of using addition												
Solves numerical problems using addition and subtraction												
Totals for each child												

Mathematics B. Using Mathematical Language

Child identifier no.	1	2	3	4	5	6	7	8	9	10	11	12
Can describe size												
Can describe position												
Recognise numbers to 10 and writes 1-10												
Can explain an addition sum												
Totals for each child												

**Family Numeracy
Tutor Questionnaire**

Please use the rating scale 1-4 with 1 representing most important and 4 least important to answer the following questions.

1. How important have each of the factors involved in the Family Numeracy project you have run been in creating effective provision for developing the parent's numeracy skills?

	1	2	3	4
Choice of curriculum content	☐	☐	☐	☐
Amount of time provision lasted (i.e. was it long enough?)	☐	☐	☐	☐
Inclusion of joint provision	☐	☐	☐	☐
Incorporating 'tasks' for home	☐	☐	☐	☐
Presence of accreditation	☐	☐	☐	☐
Pre/post testing	☐	☐	☐	☐

Any others please fill in:

_____	☐	☐	☐	☐
_____	☐	☐	☐	☐
_____	☐	☐	☐	☐

2. How important have each of the factors involved in the Family Numeracy project you have run been in increasing the parent's ability to support their children's numeracy development?

	1	2	3	4
Choice of curriculum content	☐	☐	☐	☐
Amount of time provision lasted (i.e. was it long enough?)	☐	☐	☐	☐
Inclusion of joint provision	☐	☐	☐	☐
Incorporating 'tasks' for home	☐	☐	☐	☐

Any others please fill in:

	1	2	3	4
_____	☐	☐	☐	☐
_____	☐	☐	☐	☐
_____	☐	☐	☐	☐

Name of LEA_____

Name of School_____

1. Which are the teaching approaches you have used in the Family Numeracy project which have proved effective in developing the children's numeracy skills and use and understanding of mathematical language?
(Please tick and add if necessary)

Problem solving ☐	Games ☐
Mental maths ☐	Number rhymes ☐
Role-play ☐	Number through story ☐
Construction ☐	Oral work ☐

Any others please list:

_____

_____

_____

Please use the rating scale 1-4 with 1 representing most important and 4 least important to answer the following question.

2. How important have each of the factors involved in the project you have run been in creating effective provision for developing the children's numeracy and mathematical language? *(Please tick and add if necessary)*

	1	2	3	4
Choice of curriculum content	☐	☐	☐	☐
Amount of time provision lasted (i.e. was it long enough?)	☐	☐	☐	☐
Inclusion of additional separate provision	☐	☐	☐	☐
Inclusion of joint provision	☐	☐	☐	☐

Incorporating 'tasks' for home ☐ ☐ ☐ ☐

Providing parents with the opportunity ☐ ☐ ☐ ☐
to improve their own numeracy skills

Any others please fill in:

_____ ☐ ☐ ☐ ☐

_____ ☐ ☐ ☐ ☐

_____ ☐ ☐ ☐ ☐

3. What 'spin-offs' from involvement in the Family Numeracy project would you identify for this group of children in their approach to play and work tasks? *(Please tick and add if necessary)*

Improvement in confidence ☐

Improvement in concentration and perseverance ☐

Greater cooperation and group work skills ☐

Greater eagerness to explore and initiate new learning ☐

Development of simple problem solving skills ☐

Improvement in general listening skills ☐

Improvement in listening to instructions ☐

Development in spoken vocabulary and fluency ☐

Greater interest in reading ☐

Greater interest in writing ☐

Any others please fill in:

_____

_____

_____

Name of LEA_____ Name of School_____

Family Numeracy Programme

Adult Profile

Identifier |⌷|⌷|⌷|⌷|⌷|⌷| 6-11

Gender 12

☐ Female ☐ Male

Date of birth 13-18

/ / |⌷|⌷|⌷|⌷|⌷|

Time in UK 19-22

|⌷⌷| years |⌷⌷| months

Ethnic group 23

1 ☐ White
2 ☐ Black – Caribbean
3 ☐ Black – African
4 ☐ Black – other
5 ☐ Indian
6 ☐ Pakistani
7 ☐ Bangladeshi
8 ☐ Chinese
9 ☐ Other (please specify)

Occupational Status 24

1 ☐ Full-time paid employee
2 ☐ Part-time paid employee
3 ☐ Full-time self-employed
4 ☐ Part-time self-employed
5 ☐ Unemployed
6 ☐ Full-time education
7 ☐ Temporarily sick/disabled
8 ☐ Permanently sick/disabled
9 ☐ Looking after home/family
0 ☐ Other (please specify)

Children participating on the course 25

Identifier	Date of birth	Languages	understood	spoken	literate	
_____	/ / |⌷|⌷|⌷|⌷|⌷|	_____	☐	☐	☐	
_____	/ / |⌷|⌷|⌷|⌷|⌷|	_____	☐	☐	☐	26-29
_____	/ / |⌷|⌷|⌷|⌷|⌷|	_____	☐	☐	☐	30-33
_____	/ / |⌷|⌷|⌷|⌷|⌷|	_____	☐	☐	☐	34-37
						38-41

Education

Highest mathematics qualification awarded _____ 42

Highest other qualification awarded _____ 43

Education in UK

Years in full-time education _____ 44-45 Was this continuous? ☐ Yes ☐ No (please expand) 46

Education outside UK

Years in full-time education _____ 47-48 Was this continuous? ☐ Yes ☐ No (please expand) 49

Previous basic skills tuition Yes No (please expand) 50

Family Numeracy Programme

Child Profile

Identifier ₆₋₁₁ | | | | | | | | |

Gender ¹²

☐ Female ☐ Male

Date of birth ¹³⁻¹⁸

/ /

Time in UK ¹⁹⁻²²

|_|_|_| years |_|_| months

Ethnic group ²³

¹ ☐ White

² ☐ Black – Caribbean

³ ☐ Black – African

⁴ ☐ Black – other

⁵ ☐ Indian

⁶ ☐ Pakistani

⁷ ☐ Bangladeshi

⁸ ☐ Chinese

⁹ ☐ Other (please specify)

Languages

	understood	spoken	
_____	☐	☐	24-26
_____	☐	☐	27-29
_____	☐	☐	30-32
_____	☐	☐	33-35

Does your child have experience of writing systems other than English (for example, Arabic, Chinese, Devanagari):

☐ Yes ☐ No ³⁶

If yes, please say which writing system(s) _____ ³⁷

_____ ³⁸

List of participating LEAS, schools, nurseries, family centres, etc.

THE lead partner in the Family Numeracy pilot programmes was the LEA except in two of the pilots where the lead was taken jointly by the college and the LEA and in one case by the City Council Policy Unit. The other partners included Adult Basic Skills Services within the LEA, Social Services, TECs, EBPs, Library Services, voluntary and community groups, supermarkets and other local companies.

Each pilot was awarded £10,000 and provided matched funding of at least £5,000. Some of the schools listed below hosted more than one course.

List of schools, nursery schools, family centres, playgroups and companies where the programmes were based

Cambridgeshire Local Education Authority
Peterborough College
Eyrescroft Primary School
Fulbourn Primary School
West Town Primary School

Camden Local Education Authority
Netley Primary School
Rhyl Primary School
Lyndhurst Centre
Hampden Nursery Centre

Devon Local Education Authority
Ladysmith First School
Whipton Barton First School

Dewsbury College/Kirklees Local Education Authority
Fieldhead Junior, Infant & Nursery School
Pentland County Infant School
Old Bank Junior, Infant & Nursery School

...udley College/Local Education Authority
Bromley Primary School
Brierley Primary School
Foxyards Primary School
Highfield Primary School
Sycamore Green Primary School
Wrens Nest Primary School

Gloucestershire Local Education Authority
Finlay Road Family Centre
Forest View Family Centre
Hesters Way Family Centre
The Park Family Centre

Lancashire Local Education Authority
Chorley All Saints CE Nursery School
Audley Nursery School
Deepdale County Infant School
McMillan Nursery School
Moor Nook County Primary School
Sandylane County Primary School
Shadsworth Nursery School
Skerton County Primary School
St Cuthbert's Nursery School
West Street Nursery School

Luton Education Authority
Barnfield Further Education College
Ferrars Infant School
Pastures Way Nursery School
Southfield Infant School
St Martin de Porres RC (VA) Infant School

Northamptonshire Local Education Authority
Northampton College
Tresham Institute of Further and Higher Education
Spring Lane Lower School
Rockingham Road Primary School
Pen Green Family Centre

Norfolk Local Education Authority
Bressingham Playgroup
Diss Community Playgroup
Diss Under Fives Playgroup
Garboldisham Playgroup
Gissing Playgroup
Merryfields Playgroup
Scole Pre-School
Reydon PlaygroupClover Hill First School
Cobholm First School
Costessey Infants School
Northgate St Andrews First School
St Mary's & St George's First Schools
Royal Mail

Nottingham City Council
Basford Hall College
Bonnington Infant and Primary School
Bulwell Community Toy Library
Bulwell Family Centre
Rufford Infant and Primary School

Sefton Families and Schools Together Service
Thomas Gray Infant School
St James' RC Primary School
St Monica's Primary School

Sheffield Local Education Authority
Sheffield College
Sheffield Hallam University
Arbourthorne N.I. School
Longley Primary School

South Tyneside Local Education Authority
South Tyneside College
All Saint's CE Infant School